Early Childhood Education Series

Kenneth D. Wann, Editor

NEW DIRECTIONS IN THE KINDERGARTEN

Helen F. Robison
Bernard Spodek

NEW DIRECTIONS IN THE KINDERGARTEN

Helen F. Robison

Assistant Professor of Education
Teachers College, Columbia University

Bernard Spodek

Associate Professor, College of Education
University of Illinois, Urbana, Illinois

TEACHERS COLLEGE PRESS, Teachers College,
Columbia University, New York, 1965

Cover design by Veit-Martin Associates

FOREWORD

There are many factors in the mid-1960's which make it highly appropriate to consider new directions for kindergarten education. The content and procedures of kindergarten programs have not been subjected to a thoroughgoing analysis and evaluation since the first decades of this century. After the turn of the century, leaders of the Kindergarten Reform Movement recognized that changed societal conditions and new knowledge and insights about children demanded kindergartens focused on twentieth-century children and the world in which they were to live. As a result of the analysis which followed, significant changes were made in the content and methods of kindergarten education. The gifts and occupations of the Froebelian kindergartens gave way to large blocks, doll corner equipment, and other materials emphasizing the involvement of children in an exploration of their world through dramatic play.

Children of today live in a world vastly different from that of the children of the early 1900's. It is a greatly expanded world. Children are in contact with events which occur all over this planet. They also follow with great interest the epic explorations of outer space, the moon, and other planets. Whereas children at the beginning of the century needed to understand the roles and contributions of family members and other people in their immediate communities, children today must encompass in their understandings not only their immediate surroundings but the entire world and universe as well. This need demands new emphasis and new materials in their education.

New insights about young children's learning potential give additional support for new content and procedures in kindergarten education. The growing recognition of the importance of cognitive learnings involving language and concept development during this early period further emphasize the need for careful study and definition of the direction in which kindergarten education should be moving today.

Helen Robison and Bernard Spodek have long recognized this need. While they do not advocate a complete revolution in kindergarten practices, they believe that substantial changes are in order based on careful study and analysis of children, the world in which they live and the knowledge which will contribute to children's understanding of their world. This book is the result of their careful consideration of a direction which might be taken by kindergarten educators interested in programs appropriate for today's children. It has grown from their years of experience as teachers of young children and from their systematic study and testing of new content and procedures for kindergartens.

These authors believe that the learning experiences of kindergarten children must provide the conceptual base for learnings which will be significant later as well as now. They see the possibility of appropriately beginning the development of concepts that will give greater breadth and depth to later learnings in the areas of the academic disciplines. Accordingly, they propose a way of defining goals for kindergarten education that will enable teachers to cultivate the roots of learning that will be significant to the entire life of an individual learner.

The greatest significance of this book, however, is not in the framework for defining goals, as important as this is, but in the way in which the authors have demonstrated that these learnings can be incorporated into appropriate, every-day experiences for five-year-olds. They have shown that children's need for concrete, manipulative experiences and for self-involvement in dramatic play can be utilized to bring about important learnings as they have defined them. They have shown that experiences with people, events, and materials in their immediate environment can be used to further significant language and concept development. They have demonstrated that certain kinds of direct teaching-learning experiences, when kept in careful balance with other kinds of experiences, can be fruitful and appealing to children.

The authors of this book have a vital message for kindergarten educators. Their ideas will be an invaluable help to all interested in developing kindergartens for today's children.

KENNETH D. WANN

Teachers College, Columbia University
August, 1965

CONTENTS

1

INTELLECTUAL CONTENT FOR THE KINDERGARTEN

The time has come to seek a new direction in kindergarten education. In the past few years, the need for change has been voiced by many people, including kindergarten teachers, supervisors, parents, and interested citizens. Throughout the land questions have been raised about the adequacy of the education now being offered to young children. There is anxiety that too few children are being prepared to cope with an increasingly technical and complex society. Questions about educational practices have also arisen because of the sheer mass of information that is being developed at increasingly faster rates. Changes in the nature of knowledge, in child nurture, and in the technology of our society underline the urgency to tailor programs to the needs of today's children.

In the last two decades, many new insights have been gained about the development of children in their early years. Much is known about the impact of early experiences upon the emotional and intellectual life of the child. These insights, interpreted and understood in the context of modern society, can contribute to defining a kindergarten curriculum that will help children move toward greater understanding of the world in which they live. This can take place without forsaking the positive mental health practices that have been developed in kindergarten programs.

To be sure, the kindergarten must continue to be a place where children are happy, but it must also be a place where children are helped to deal with significant ideas about their physical and social world. The young child has a right to a kindergarten where he can deal with ideas that are important and significant and where he can be helped to grapple with these on his own terms. Such a kindergarten would provide learning, not "prelearning," experience and would therefore be the real beginning and foundation of all his later learning.

This new direction does not necessarily call for a complete revolution in kindergarten practices. Determination of the new direction should flow from an analysis of the theories and ideas that underly all good educational practices and from knowledge of the life of the modern child. It calls upon the tradition of the pioneers of the kindergarten whose message is still timely today:

> The kindergarten will grow in value as our vision of life and our insight into the meaning of education deepen and broaden. It will be altered from year to year by reflection upon what we have attempted and what we have accomplished. Out of this will come a new vision, a higher standard which will enable us to reconstruct and create newer and more ideal courses of study for the children of the future.[1]

There are changes in children's early experiences and maturation today that should be mirrored by changes in the educational experiences they are offered. Children's physical maturation is accelerating because of excellent prenatal and infant care and for other reasons. More children live in urban settings with increasingly mobile populations. The prevalence of the automobile has made the experiences of today's children markedly different from those of a generation ago. For many families, travel has become the rule rather than the exception. For increasing numbers of children, the kindergarten is no longer the first educational experience away from home as more children are enrolled in nursery schools and day care centers.

The impact of television has meant a different pattern of living for all children from that of their parents. Research studies have documented the impact of this medium on young children. Earlier vocabulary development and increased familiarity with current events, local and worldwide, have been among the most widely noted effects of children's televiewing.

Existing kindergarten practices are sometimes defended as a

[1] Patty Smith Hill, "Second Report," *The Kindergarten*, Boston: Houghton Mifflin, 1913, pp. 274–275.

protection of the kindergarten child's right to be five. However, what a child is at five is determined to no small extent by his cultural environment. Childhood experiences are different in each society and at different times in history. Schools must deal with the child as he is today, helping to prepare him to cope with the world as it is and as it seems likely to be.

CONTENT FOR THE
KINDERGARTEN PROGRAM

The central problem in kindergarten education today is its content. In the recent past, educators of young children regarded "content-oriented" teachers with suspicion because they were assumed to be necessarily more preoccupied with things and ideas than with children. The prevailing emphasis in kindergarten education has been on experiences and activities, with content largely undefined. Classroom teachers chose content as they sensed interest among the children or as their personal inclinations directed. Generally, kindergarten content was in terms of vague, slogan-like goals, and there was no demonstrable relationship between the specific learning activities the teacher initiated and any such expected learnings. Challenged by a parent or uninformed visitor to describe her curriculum, the kindergarten teacher was likely to reply in terms of her "child development" approach to teaching five-year-olds.

Contributions of the Developmental Approach

Content was largely removed from early childhood education by prevalent misinterpretations of what developmental psychology required in teaching young children. Educators of young children understood "child development" as an approach to their physical, social, and emotional growth. While intellectual growth was always added to the list, teachers' concerns for social and emotional growth were regarded as primary, with intellectual growth as an expected result but requiring little of the teacher's time in planning and programming. This emphasis on the child's emotional and social growth was actually a most beneficial one for a time, serving to balance previous ignorance of the powerful effects of children's emotional stresses and problems upon their interest and ability to learn. However, a new imbalance was created in which children's need for intellectual content was largely ignored.

There is growing interest today in restoring balance to the kindergarten curriculum, and much interest now centers on content and bases for its selection. Certain developmental psychologists have been trying to correct widespread misconceptions about the "child development" point of view in curriculum design. Often, teachers have stated that the child development approach furnishes the content for the program; however, developmental psychologists point out that this is not possible. Developmental learning, they say, is concerned with the ways in which children deal with information and concepts, but it cannot dictate the content from which children gather information and begin to conceptualize.[2] The child development approach helps teachers to distinguish between effective and ineffective learning methods and teachers' approaches to children which foster learning and those that do not.

If developmental psychology indicates that young children must first deal with the most physical and concrete aspects of reality before they can go on to symbolization, representation, and abstraction, curriculum designers have still to identify the most appropriate areas of reality to study, that is, the specific content.

Many educators of young children have expressed concern that systematic introduction of content will result in "pushing" children too early into formal instruction or into parroting facts they do not comprehend. This concern must be viewed as substantial and worthy of consideration. Unfortunately, there are schools in which parents' desire for better education of young children has resulted in inappropriate formal reading programs and workbook exercises. Some of these programs may be quite irrelevant to the young child's basic educational needs, while others may be positively harmful and damaging to his further educational progress.

Fears that intellectual development of young children will be pursued through undesirable programs should galvanize educators

[2] Dale B. Harris, "Child Development," in American Association of Colleges for Teacher Education, *Recent Research and Developments and Their Implications for Teacher Education*, Thirteenth Yearbook, Chicago: National Education Association, 1960, pp. 28–44.

of young children to devise better alternatives. Educators cannot protect children from change. However, educators can help to determine the nature of the curricular changes indicated, while preserving desirable practices which stem from developmental psychology. This would mean the construction of programs which help the child to move ahead in intellectual learnings that are stimulating and that will help him to develop his thinking and reasoning abilities. Good content selection should facilitate this process. Fears that intellectual stimulation per se, through deliberate content selection, might be damaging to young children are contradicted by considerable psychological research and theory. White's theory of competence motivation stresses the feelings of mastery and competence which children derive from experimental efforts to satisfy curiosity.[3] According to White, children require stimulation and regular opportunities for environmental exploration in order to experience cognitive satisfaction.

Content Selection in the Past

The plea for content in the kindergarten curriculum which will be intellectually stimulating is not new but has been stated in different ways by kindergarten educators at different periods. The dilemma has always been to mediate between the child's present understandings, which are rather primitive at the kindergarten level, and the sophistication of organized knowledge. These have often been seen as so different as to preclude meaningful interaction. Dewey, however, saw the role of the school as unifying societal knowledge with the child's ability to assimilate it meaningfully:

It is just to get rid of the prejudicial notion that there is some gap in kind (as distinct from degree) between the child's experience and the various forms of subject-matter that make up the course of study. From the side of the child, it is a question of seeking how his experience already contains within itself elements—facts and truths—of just the same sort as those entering into the formulated study; and, what is of more importance, of how it contains within itself the attitudes, the motives and the interests which have operated in developing and organizing the subject matter to the plane which it now occupies. From the side of the studies

[3] Robert F. White, "Motivation Reconsidered: The Concept of Competence," *Psychological Review*, 1959, 66(5):297–333.

it is a question of interpreting them as outgrowths of forces operating in the child's life and of discovering the steps that intervene between the child's present experience and their richer maturity.[4]

To discover these "steps that intervene" is the prime function of teachers at all levels, to help children advance toward the acquisition of knowledge and efficient modes of thinking. This view, then, regards the teacher as the mediator between the child's present stage of development and the organized body of knowledge that the child has to attain. In this attainment of knowledge the kindergarten can play an important role. The decision about content must rest not only upon factors of child development but also upon the nature of the knowledge to be learned and upon the state of the teaching arts, as well.

Content Problems Today

Dissatisfaction with the content of kindergarten programs for today's children stems largely from the incidental, haphazard, accidental basis for selection, inherent in the "emerging" curriculum. The "emerging" curriculum idea, with its insistence that only those experiences which "emerge" from day-to-day living will have meaning to children, is becoming increasingly difficult to defend. If children can deal with ideas and derive pleasure as well as learning from appropriate activities, there seems no sound reason to avoid planning specific content selection. Yet the assumption of the "emerging" curriculum, that the child is the one who is best equipped to judge which ideas he can handle and to initiate his own learning, prevents teacher planning and selection of content. It restricts the child's learning opportunities to his own immature perceptions and understandings of the realities of the world.

Sometimes the kindergarten program, in attempting to deal only with ideas that appear to be within the child's experience, strikes unexpected snags. For example, most kindergartens have daily programs for marking the calendar and for taking attendance. In both cases, abstract and uncomprehended concepts of counting and

[4] John Dewey, *The Child and The Curriculum*, Chicago: University of Chicago Press, 1902, pp. 15–16.

of time are dealt with in rather abstract terms. The mathematical concepts are well worth developing, but not in the vague, rote fashion in which they are usually handled. Five-year-olds who have not yet mastered groups within five are frequently asked to "add" twelve boys, thirteen girls, a teacher, and a visitor or two. The counting is seldom based on a one-to-one correspondence, nor is grouping within tens ever attempted. The calendar marking, usually, is purely by rote.

To defend the study of abstract and advanced concepts such as those cited above while rejecting carefully planned studies of mathematics concepts based on concrete, manipulative objects seems contradictory. If children are to comprehend thirty days in a month or twenty-seven people in attendance, more basic number studies seem essential as prior experience.

Sheer complexity need not be the basis for rejection of concepts to study, either. If it seems desirable to help children form a working understanding of concepts which are complicated, the remedy lies not in putting off learning experiences but in shaping experiences so that initial learnings can be achieved, upon which more complex understandings can be built. The conventional interpretation of "here and now" content for young children seems less fruitful than other ways of defining content.

The interest in new programs for young children has engendered serious thinking about how content can be selected for their use and what elements of content in various fields are especially relevant, basic, and essential to later learning.

Need for Intellectual Content

Recent research and newer views of children's cognitive abilities and needs are now firmly supporting the young child's need for intellectual content in school programs. Hunt suggests the need to govern the encounters children have with the environment, in order to help children practice and develop their maturing abilities.[5] It is his view that early experience for perceptual and intellectual functions is of basic importance because stunted intellectual growth seems so

[5] J. McV. Hunt, *Intelligence and Experience*, New York: Ronald Press, 1961.

difficult to reverse.[6] Almy, too, has stressed the child's need for rich stimulation and experience to advance his transition from simpler to more complex levels of thinking.[7] Psychologists today are much concerned with the role of experience in the intellectual development of disadvantaged children and they do not expect that optimum growth will occur by chance for these children.

Wann's recent study of young children's attempts to understand their environment indicated a surprisingly wide scope for their intellectual interests. According to Wann, "the readiness and need for young children to organize and see relationships among their observations of the world around them points to concept development as a key element in selection."[8] The urgency of the need of all children for a conceptual framework for dealing with the world underlines the significance of current proposals for content selection.

A PROPOSAL FOR
SELECTION OF CONTENT

Before we can have good content selection, we must have a way of identifying content that will be meaningful to young children and significant in extending and challenging their understanding of their world. We must identify content that will foster a fruitful way of thinking about the world and provide a base for interpreting and understanding the child's continuous encounters with the social and physical world.

One promising proposal for content selection is the "structure of the disciplines" approach. This is the plan to identify the key

[6] J. McV. Hunt, "The Psychological Basis for Using Pre-School Enrichment as an Antidote for Cultural Deprivation," *Merrill-Palmer Quarterly of Behavior and Development*, 1964, 10(3):209–248.

[7] Millie Almy, "New Views on Intellectual Development: A Renaissance for Early Childhood Education," in A. Harry Passow and Robert R. Leeper (Eds.), *Intellectual Development: Another Look* (papers from the ASCD Eighth Curriculum Research Institute), Washington, D.C.: Association for Supervision and Curriculum Development, 1964, pp. 12–26.

[8] Kenneth D. Wann, Miriam Selchen Dorn, and Elizabeth Ann Liddle, *Fostering Intellectual Development in Young Children*, New York: Teachers College Press, Teachers College, Columbia University, 1962, p. 117.

concepts in each major discipline or body of knowledge as the content for children to learn.[9] According to this proposal, the academic scholar in each major discipline, either alone or in collaboration with educators, would identify and select the key concepts or big ideas in his own field. In addition to delineating these major conceptualizations in a body of knowledge, scholars would also identify basic relationships within the conceptual framework. Finally, these scholars would specify the fundamental ways of acquiring knowledge, or of verifying knowledge, which are characteristic of each discipline, as for example the "historical method" in historical research. The identification of key concepts, together with the major relationships among these concepts and the ways of acquiring or confirming new knowledge in a discipline, is regarded as the structure of the discipline.

It is important to recognize that this proposal leaves teaching in the hands of teachers. It is not implied that teachers will learn more about teaching methodology from mathematicians or historians. But this proposal seeks to make available to teachers clearer and more authoritative material regarding the important ideas in each body of knowledge, so that teachers will have more significant and worthwhile goals for their teaching.

The content would be selected for teachers only in terms of the big ideas in each body of knowledge. Teachers and curriculum workers would start with this broad content and from it they would elaborate and specify some of the understandings children would have to develop before they could be expected to grasp these big ideas clearly. This could result in a series of hierarchical ideas, very simple translations of the big ideas for the youngest grades in school, with gradually increasing complexity and interrelationships introduced at succeeding school levels. Actually, in some disciplines, scholars have sought to prepare for teachers the entire hierarchy of ideas to be learned by children, from the first early understandings to the full-fledged abstractions in the discipline. In whatever form

[9] See Philip H. Phenix, "Key Concepts and the Crisis in Learning," *Teachers College Record*, 1956, 58:137–143; Arthur W. Foshay, "A Modest Proposal," *Educational Leadership*, 1961, 18:506–516; and Jerome S. Bruner, *The Process of Education*, Cambridge, Mass.: Harvard University Press, 1960.

this package of content is delivered to teachers, it could become the basis for program planning over long periods of time, sometimes throughout the child's school career.

The importance of the child's construction, or development, of basic concepts lies in the economy and permanence of learning which can result. That children are constantly gathering information is well known to all educators. The more perceptive the child, the more items and details he notes and remembers. But masses of information and detail can be meaningless to the young child. He is often unable to make sense out of his information, to relate one piece of information to another, to classify like pieces of information together or to distinguish between unlike items on relevant criteria. The child's construction of basic concepts could provide the niches needed for sorting different kinds of information, for labeling and identifying meanings, for comparing items of information for their relevance to concepts or for needed changes in conceptualization. Details are easily forgotten, but meanings tend to have permanence and stability; thus, conceptual learning contributes to life-long understanding. Furthermore, the learning of concepts and relationships leads to the possibilities of more complex thinking, of dealing with generalizations and abstractions instead of concrete items. Therefore, programs which promote conceptual learning may contribute to the development of the complex intellectual thinking needed for today's success in school and in life.

An example of how conceptual learning can facilitate understanding and intellectual progress for an adult may clarify its possibilities for children. A first-grade teacher in a graduate course was trying to understand decimal base by constructing a number system to other bases, such as 2 or 9, despite her distaste for mathematics. Suddenly she discovered some meanings and relationships which had heretofore eluded her, that is, the relationship of the units to the tens column, the relationship of tens to hundreds, and so on. Extracting the concept and applying it to nondecimal bases, this teacher found satisfaction in her mastery of the idea and her ability to use it. Her cry, "Why didn't anybody ever tell me this before?" underlines the need to help children to discover meaning earlier in life, before frustration and confusion block learning and the will to learn.

Concept Learning in the Kindergarten

In the kindergarten, the learning of key concepts could become the intellectual goals of the grade, supplementing physical, social, and emotional goals. The content would be developed through instructional materials and experiences from which young children could be expected to gather information, ideas, skills and attitudes. While the teacher would not be explicitly teaching the basic concepts which she hopes the children will learn, she would be exerting her skill in making available to them selected areas of information and experience and helping children to make sense out of their assorted collections of data. Without teaching reading and without formal instruction, the teacher would encourage and stimulate children's interests and efforts, thus helping them perceive and conceptualize more clearly.

Experiences, materials, and equipment would be selected and used in ways which seem likely to help children find the meanings and relationships selected for learning. Instead of taking children on loosely planned trips to encourage as-yet-undefined learnings, the teacher will now be encouraged to plan a trip because of some specific data she wishes the children to perceive and experience, in order to build a base for the concepts she wants them to construct. She is not required to inhibit children in any exploratory activities of their own devising. She offers more possibilities than most children could initiate, and she is purposeful in her efforts to help children to move out of ruts and blind alleys into the broad thoroughfare of accumulated knowledge and ideas.

The children's active involvement in manipulative, exploratory, varying experiences would be a major learning avenue, with strong emphasis upon play and individual choice. To this, the teacher would add stimulating and suggestive materials, direction, support, verbalization and clarification, practice activities, and interaction. Learnings could be expected to vary, and children's individual progress would be evaluated with the same sympathetic understanding accorded learnings of a physical or social nature.

Basic to this suggested approach is the assumption that lists of unrelated facts can be neither remembered nor related to other information when needed. A student's understanding of the major ideas in a body of knowledge can provide a framework of understanding. With this framework, he can store facts, retrieving them when needed in connection with the ideas involved. If the student learns not only the key concepts but the ways in which new knowledge is confirmed or acquired, he is thought to be developing a life-long way to keep on learning and to keep up with new knowledge as it is discovered.

In 1960 Bruner popularized this proposal for curriculum change in his book, *The Process of Education*, stating that any subject can be taught in some intellectually honest form to any child at any age.[10] Bruner envisioned a curriculum based, at all grade levels, on the same basic set of ideas:

> Surely all this argues for something akin to a spiral curriculum in which ideas are first presented in a form and language, honest though imprecise, which can be grasped by the child, ideas that can be revisited later with greater precision and power until, finally, the student has achieved the reward of mastery.[11]

He suggested that the development of the general idea

> . . . comes first from a first round of experience with concrete embodiments of ideas that are close to a child's life. The cycle of learning begins, then, with particulars and immediately moves toward abstraction. It comes to a temporary goal when the abstraction can be used in grasping new particulars in the deeper way that abstraction permits.[12]

The major roadblock to achieving such a curriculum is the difficulty in securing a systematic, authoritative delineation of the major ideas in all the content areas with their unique ways of knowing. A second barrier consists in the difficulty early childhood specialists have in visualizing a program which could accomplish these promised benefits without doing violence to well-established principles of good kindergarten programs.

It must be stressed that the key concepts in any body of knowledge are not meant to be taught directly to children. These are meant to be the ideas which children are expected to discover or to formulate from the meaningful educational experiences offered

---

[10] Jerome S. Bruner, *op. cit.*, p. 12.

[11] Jerome S. Bruner, *On Knowing*, Cambridge, Mass.: The Belknap Press of Harvard University Press, 1962, p. 24.

[12] *Ibid.*, p. 123.

throughout the school grades, with the active guidance of knowledgeable teachers. In the lower grades, instead of learning some isolated facts, children would be offered experiences and materials from which they would be expected to grasp rough approximations of some of the more complicated concepts and perhaps some precise understandings of some of the simpler ones. Decisions about what to teach would be geared to facilitating children's gaining these understandings.

There are many advantages for curriculum development and for teachers in this proposal. The leadership of academic scholars or their collaboration with educators in defining the basic ideas in each body of knowledge insures authoritative and significant results. Such a listing of key concepts may become the goal of all grade levels in a content area, although with increasing complexity at higher grades. While the same basic concepts can be interpreted for any given grade level or for any specific group of children, it provides a basic unity in children's learning of each content area throughout the school. The kindergarten and primary grades are just as important as the later grades in conceptual learning, especially because good beginnings of basic concepts are to be established upon which subsequent learnings can be built. Instead of coping with a curriculum unrelated to later school learning, kindergarten children would be beginning to fashion the basic concepts they will be expanding and developing all through school.

For teachers, this proposal presents an understandable and logical basis for programming, one which can be rationally developed and initiated, in contrast to the vague, intuitive, accidental base which so many teachers have found unsatisfactory. It offers kindergarten teachers greater community of interest with other teachers, opportunities to work on a schoolwide basis for allocation of content material to different grade levels and the certainty that children will have later opportunities to continue to learn ideas which need time and further study. Since this proposal does not prescribe how the concepts are to be constructed by the children, teachers will find continued freedom to exercise creativity in programming. Neither does the proposal require any one teaching methodology; it encompasses the present wide range now in use, from considerable free choices for children to highly directed activities.

Since the kindergarten program does not require reading instruction, it can challenge children of varying abilities, from the deprived and slower children to the gifted. With more children involved in self-selected learning activities which offer satisfaction and meaningful activity, teachers should find less boredom and fewer disciplinary problems than in a conventional program.

TESTING THE PROPOSAL
IN THE KINDERGARTEN

Teachers who are interested in trying out a curriculum based on the ideas proposed here will find statements of key concepts lacking in many areas. This was the experience of the authors of this book when they set out to test these ideas in a kindergarten classroom. Their experience indicates the possibility of developing tentative statements of key concepts that can be the basis for experimental programs. The interest aroused in this approach is stimulating the production of more statements of key concepts by scholars in the various disciplines. All such statements, including the most authoritative ones, can be regarded as tentative and subject to change. In fact, modern life imposes a view of all knowledge as tentatively understood and subject to revision.

The authors of this book, finding themselves dissatisfied with the intellectual content of conventional kindergarten programs, independently undertook two studies to test whether kindergarten children could learn some meaningful beginning concepts within a discipline or body of knowledge. These studies are described in Chapters 2 and 3. Changing views on young children's cognitive abilities and needs and Wann's study emphasizing young children's intellectual interests and abilities indicated the need for testing some new programs which could have significance for the young child. Articulation with children's later school experiences was an additional goal. Earlier reading instruction and wholesale "downgrading" of content from the first grade to the kindergarten did not seem to be the answer to the needs of five-year-olds. Bruner's adventurous suggestion that even young children could begin to learn significant concepts in some primitive form added further inspiration. If the new proposal to direct the curriculum to the learning of key concepts in content areas could offer worthwhile learnings in a continuously expanding and growing program to older children, why not in the kindergarten? If this new program proved practical for five-year-olds, it would furnish an organizing basis for the kindergarten curriculum, which has so far been lacking, that would be in harmony with that of the school generally.

Emphasizing children's efforts in active exploration and discovery, as Bruner did, for the learning of key concepts and ways of acquiring knowledge, made this proposal especially consonant with young children's ways of learning.

In their respective studies, the authors of this book also stressed young children's manipulation of objects and spontaneous activity as primary learning techniques. Both were interested in evaluating experiences, materials, and methods used for promoting the desired learning. The studies, which took place in the same classroom in successive years, tested kindergarten children's learning of some concepts in history and geography the first year and in economics the second year.

One reason for the selection of these areas of social science was that the enduring character of the issues, principles, and values involved makes these disciplines worthy of study by young children. Another was the likelihood of early introduction to information from these content areas through the child's own experience, through television and other mass media, and through the adults closest to him. Early study of these areas could also contribute to children's beginning to understand their world and to constructing some concepts and ways of thinking with which they will be dealing throughout their lives. Thus, these are bodies of knowledge which have both present significance for the young child and continuing significance for the mature adult.

A third reason for the selections made was the likelihood of there being—in these content areas—concrete experiences close to a child's life, so that school instruction could build upon children's prior experience. Many facets of children's lives are directly touched by the economics of buying and selling, of family income and employment and other basic economic factors. Similarly, children have since birth been direct observers of much geographical phenomena so that continuity is readily attained and maintained on a

level of concreteness and physical reality. History may seem somewhat removed from a young child's experience on first thought, but
on closer analysis it becomes apparent that the child experiences
some historical phenomena and change even though he is not
conscious of this experience or of the possibility of viewing his
experiences this way.

Both studies were conducted in the kindergarten of the Agnes
Russell School at Teachers College, Columbia University. This is
not a laboratory school but a service school for children of a
university community, housed in an old building which was not
designed for its present use. The classroom was somewhat small for
its average enrollment of twenty-five children and was not as well
equipped as most public school kindergartens. The class, which met
only in the morning, had access to a rooftop playground, a basement
pool for weekly swims, a gymnasium for work with the physical
education instructor, and a children's library for sessions on children's literature with a consultant. In other respects, the program
was quite conventional.

The role of the researcher in the classroom alternated from
planning and coteaching, by prearrangement with the teacher, to
observing and recording children's behavior. In addition to working
with some or all of the children along planned lines on occasion,
the researcher also acted as a resource person to the teacher with
respect to the social science concepts only.

FINDINGS OF STUDIES
OF CONCEPT LEARNING

In both studies, while there was the expected variety in concept
development among the children, it was clear that conceptual
progress was directly determined by the educational opportunities
offered in the programs. Control data in both studies indicated that
the significant progress made by the children could not have been
attributed to maturation or to everyday experience.

The studies showed it was possible to organize learning experiences in the kindergarten into discrete episodes which extend over a
long period of time. In neither study was there a sequential and
continuous series of encounters with the concepts selected for study.

Episodes were periodic in the geography–history study, occurring every week or two, but there was no regularity to the timing of the experiences in the economics study. In both studies there was explicit acceptance of the growth ideal in young children's gradually developing concepts growing out of revisiting ideas in different contexts over a substantial period of time.

The studies indicated that intellectual learning could be pursued by children chiefly through established kindergarten experiences and activities, without imposing new restraints or formalities upon young children. The children gathered information and insights in a variety of ways through different media. They utilized pieces of information, testing, organizing, and modifying understandings through many different experiences. Meeting information and ideas in different contexts and through different kinds of experiences contributed to children's growing efforts to categorize, classify, and conceptualize.

This new direction in kindergarten education offers rich potential for all children's early education. All children can use more intellectual content for their serious efforts to structure reality, which adults call play. Teachers can find more purpose and direction for curriculum development in clear goals stated as key concepts to be learned. Many questions remain in the development of the kindergarten curriculum in this new direction and the many problems and possibilities which must be considered are discussed in the remaining sections of this book.

BIBLIOGRAPHY

Almy, Millie, "New Views on Intellectual Development: A Renaissance for Early Childhood Education," in A. Harry Passow and Robert R. Leeper (Eds.), *Intellectual Development: Another Look* (papers from the ASCD Eighth Curriculum Research Institute), Washington, D.C.: Association for Supervision and Curriculum Development, 1964, pp. 12–26.

Bruner, Jerome S., *The Process of Education*, Cambridge, Mass.: Harvard University Press, 1960.

———, *On Knowing*, Cambridge, Mass.: Belknap Press of Harvard University Press, 1962.

Dewey, John, *The Child and The Curriculum*, Chicago: University of Chicago Press, 1902.

Foshay, Arthur W., "A Modest Proposal," *Educational Leadership*, 1961, 18:506–516.

Harris, Dale B., "Child Development," in American Association of Colleges for Teacher Education, *Recent Research and Developments and Their Implications for Teacher Education*, Thirteenth Yearbook, Chicago: National Education Association, 1960, pp. 28–44.

Hill, Patty Smith, "Second Report," *The Kindergarten*, Boston: Houghton Mifflin, 1913.

Hunt, J. McV., *Intelligence and Experience*, New York: Ronald Press, 1961.

———, "The Psychological Basis for Using Pre-School Enrichment as an Antidote for Cultural Deprivation," *Merrill-Palmer Quarterly of Behavior and Development*, 1964, 10(3):209–248.

National Task Force on Economic Education, *Economic Education in the Schools*, New York: Committee for Economic Development, 1961.

Phenix, Philip H., "Key Concepts and the Crisis in Learning," *Teachers College Record*, 1956, 58:137–143.

Spodek, Bernard, and Helen F. Robison, "Are Kindergartens Obsolete?" *Elementary School Journal*, 1965, 65(6):300–305.

Wann, Kenneth D., Miriam Selchen Dorn, and Elizabeth Ann Liddle, *Fostering Intellectual Development in Young Children*, New York: Teachers College Press, Teachers College, Columbia University, 1962.

White, Robert F., "Motivation Reconsidered: The Concept of Competence," *Psychological Review*, 1959, 66(5):297–333.

2

GEOGRAPHY AND HISTORY CONCEPTS IN THE KINDERGARTEN

The idea of introducing geographic and historical concepts to kindergarten children is not new. Substantial beginnings had been achieved by such innovators in early childhood education as Lucy Sprague Mitchell[1] and Caroline Pratt.[2] It had been their clear conviction that five-year-olds could deal with important aspects of reality if only teachers could select or develop experiences and materials from which understandings could grow. Today, the innovator is faced once more with decisions as to which understandings are basic to further learning and of significance to the child, as well as what kinds of programs can achieve these goals for today's children. What important aspects of reality can a five-year-old be expected to learn, and how can the teacher plan for this learning to take place?

One effort to discover some of the possibilities as well as the limitations of working with five-year-old children in the understanding of key concepts centered on some basic understandings in geography and history.[3] This work on the development of historical and geographic concepts extended over a period of two-and-a-half months and was organized in a spiral fashion. Activities were

[1] Lucy Sprague Mitchell, *Here and Now Storybook*, New York: E. P. Dutton, 1921; *Young Geographers*, New York: John Day, 1934.

[2] Caroline Pratt, *Experimental Practices in City and Country School*, New York: E. P. Dutton, 1924.

[3] Bernard Spodek, "Developing Social Science Concepts in the Kindergarten," unpublished Ed.D. Project, Teachers College, Columbia University, 1962.

provided to present basic ideas to the children. These same ideas, in addition to new ones, were presented at intervals in the program through a variety of activities. In this way, it was thought, children could develop new understandings and expand those already attained, while returning to and reinforcing previous understandings. The spiral organization of the program assumed the gradual growth of concepts and children's continuing integration of information and ideas into increasingly complex levels of understanding.

SOURCES OF
THE PROGRAM

In order to develop a program based upon the important concepts from geography and history, it was necessary to locate or identify these concepts first. Then, these abstractions had to be translated into simply stated understandings which could be grasped by five-year-olds. The next step was to determine a topic for the study around which many different understandings could be explored. Many different topics, equally fruitful, could have been selected. Finally, a series of experiences had to be planned which could lead to children's learning of the selected understandings and needed material had to be provided.

A survey of social science textbooks, curriculum guides, and courses of study used by many school systems indicated that these were not adequate sources of concepts. In the field of economics the first step had already been taken by scholars who were attempting to define the basic concepts to be taught in the high schools. A statement of these concepts developed by the National Task Force on Economic Education in 1961 became the basis for the economic study (see Chapter 3). The lack of such a statement required additional effort in the geography–history study to identify some basic ideas in these areas.

At the time the geography–history study was begun, scholars in these areas were not yet delving into the "structure" of their disciplines to identify key concepts that could be used in developing educational programs. Therefore, the researcher conferred personally with specialists in history and geography education to discuss basic concepts and the ways in which these specialists might study New York as a harbor, the topic chosen as the focus for this study.

These conferences led to a statement of more specific concepts about New York as a harbor, as for example:

A. Man can understand the geographic aspects of a harbor by analyzing the following factors:
  1. Site—The physical characteristics.
  2. Situation—The relationship of the harbor to its service area.
  3. Facilities—The facilities necessary for functioning as a harbor.
  4. Functions—The interrelationship of the harbor and other functions of the city.
B. Man is able to represent the world and its parts symbolically.
C. Man can place occurring events in a framework of chronological time.
D. Changes that have taken place in the harbor can be understood in relation to changes in technology and the needs of the people.
E. These changes can be understood in the framework of time and space.

Under each of these headings was placed a list of specific understandings about *New York as a Harbor*, which became the goal of the program. These understandings were as follows:

1. Manhattan is an island, completely surrounded by water.

2. Because it is an island, it is crowded. Buildings are high, and bridges and tunnels are needed for people to get on and off Manhattan.

3. People go to and from work in New York in different ways.

4. Ocean-going boats can enter the Port of New York alone, but they need tugboats to help them dock.

5. Even in winter boats can go in and out of New York.

6. Boats come from great distances to New York.

7. Many of the goods and people entering New York come by means of transportation other than boat.

8. Many of the goods and people entering New York by boat are transferred to other means of transportation and leave the city.

9. There are many different kinds of boats.

10. Boats carry cargo and people.

11. Different boats perform different services.

12. Boats are different today than they were long ago.

13. A boat is a community. There are different jobs that different people do on boats.

14. Boats use different means of communication with each other and with the land.

15. Areas in the city can be located by distance and direction.

16. A picture can be drawn to represent different parts of the land. This picture, using scale, distance, and direction, is called a map.

17. Boats use maps (or charts) and compasses to travel on the ocean.

18. Tides in New York cause the level of the water to rise and fall.

19. Boats dock on the shores of Manhattan and on opposite shores.

20. Time can be measured in many ways. We use time in understanding the long-ago.

Although the ideas the children were expected to develop were organized by the researcher in logical fashion, the program did not follow any such sequential order. The same ideas were approached in many different ways through many different activities. Unrelated ideas were sometimes studied at the same time. But the program offered the children ample time and occasions to think about, explore, play with, and grasp ideas. Although the general direction of the program was developed in advance, decisions about many of the specific activities and the timing of these activities were left open, to be made as the impact of the program on the children's learning became apparent.

Considerable flexibility in detailed scheduling was combined with precise, long-range planning of a series of episodes over a long enough period of time for children to begin to grasp the desired concepts. The voluntary character of the planned activities was emphasized by the many free choices available to the children in a well-balanced, daily program. There was no plan for continuous, uninterrupted scheduling, and the results did not indicate any ill-effects from this episodic scheduling. On the contrary, episodic learning seemed well adapted to young children's growing and changing learning patterns. The specific aspects of the program described in the following sections of this chapter will illustrate how the program developed from day to day.

MAP CONCEPTS

Because maps are important in the study of geography, specific map concepts had to be developed in this program. The children needed to learn some basic ideas about distance, direction, and scale. They also had to develop the skills needed to relate a map to a geographic area, to locate places using distance and direction, and to abstract information from map symbols. Since maps are the tools of the geographer, an understanding of these symbols was essential for children's comprehension of geographic information.

Introducing Maps

At the beginning of the study an attempt was made to find out if the children had any knowledge of maps. The children were shown a map of the New York City area and were asked what it was. Among the answers received were:

"A map."

"It shows you where you're supposed to go."

"It shows you roads. It helps you ride."

"It shows you rivers."

"It shows you where the bridges are and it shows you where you are going."

Later in the discussion another child defined a map as, "a picture of part of the world."

The map which was used, although relatively uncomplicated, showed the land area symbolized by a single color while the water was symbolized by two shades of blue, each representing a different range of water depth. This latter difference in shading caused some confusion for the children. The land was easily identified but, since the children knew no reasons for showing water in two different colors, they tended to make unrealistic differentiations such as:

"The dock and the ocean."

"The ocean and the sea."

"The ocean and the beach."

Although the children lacked the information needed to understand the symbolic use of color, they did conceive of these areas in geographic terms. Navigational channels in the river were marked on this map. These were identified by some children as roads, bridges, or tunnels. In both these cases the children were attempting to deal with new symbols on this particular map by generalizing from prior experiences, such as interpretation of road maps.

In these first discussions about maps, it was quickly apparent that the children had a fund of knowledge to which they could relate new understandings of maps and geographic concepts. In a further attempt to test the depth of the children's understanding of map representation, they were provided with an opportunity to map a small area that was well known to them, that is, the kindergarten classroom. A floor plan rests upon much the same concept of representation. Floor plans were discussed with the children. It was pointed out that in making a floor plan one must draw objects as seen from above. The discussion covered the objects that would be included in a floor plan and then the children were asked to draw their own floor plans of the room.

An analysis of the children's drawings showed that most of them simply drew the furniture in the room, as seen from the child's eye level, along the bottom of the sheet of paper. One child, who drew a floor plan of his own room at home, came close to developing a true floor plan. He ranged the objects over the entire page, putting each object in a logical relationship to others. He also drew the tops of objects. The legs of the furniture, however, jutted out from each edge, rather than being hidden from view. There was some evidence that children did understand the ideas underlying floor plans. Nevertheless, they were not able to produce such representations themselves. It is interesting to note that even at the end of the study, the children had not developed this skill, though they had many experiences with maps. It seemed too difficult for them to visualize a room from the ceiling looking down.

Many kinds of representations were used in helping children understand maps. Conventional maps and floor plans constituted two different types. Another type of representation was provided through unit blocks. As it developed, these unit blocks were much more understandable and useful to the children as a form of representation than either the floor plans or the maps. Blocks were easily manipulated by children, so that representations were readily constructed without any of the demanding skills needed for drawing maps and floor plans. They enabled children to construct three-dimensional representations while showing spatial relationships. Blocks also provided the children with expanding play possibilities after the representations were constructed. Evolving and expanding play helped children understand the interrelationships of elements in the geographic area under study. Blocks also permit construction with considerable creativity and individuality along with reasonable fidelity to reality.

Block Representation of Geographic Areas

The school in which this study took place was near the Hudson River. The children were taken to the river one day to see the boats. Upon returning from this trip, the teacher taped a long strip of blue shelf paper to the floor in the block area. She told the children that this could represent the river. It was suggested that the children use blocks to build structures along this "river." Small plastic boats were provided for the play. The block construction which developed was permitted to remain intact over a period of several days in order that the children could continue their play.

At first the children simply sailed the toy boats up and down the shelf paper river. After a while, one child remarked, "We need someplace to go."

"Why don't you build a dock?" suggested the teacher.

Several children joined in building the dock. Shortly after that, another child commented: "I need a bridge." And so a bridge was built.

Slowly, as the children's play shuttled between fantasy and reality, a representation of a river with docks, bridges, and warehouses developed. Soon the bridge was connected with a block roadway to an airport. Shortly, a beehive of activity was seen. Boats were sailing up and down the river, cars and trucks were driving along the road and over the bridge, and airplanes were taking off and landing at the airport. Through all this activity the docks and bridges were extended, torn down, and rebuilt. The children's block play indicated the threads of understanding of geographic representations and relationships which were being developed.

Using Unplanned Experiences

Unplanned experiences can be used to further the goals of the program when these goals are sufficiently clear and specific to guide the teacher. Sensitive teachers can utilize many of the incidental happenings in the kindergarten to enrich and extend the understandings of children in an area being studied. There were a number of occasions in this study when unplanned experiences provided opportunities to help children extend their growing geography and history concepts.

As the program continued, there were a few days when the teacher was absent due to illness. Although the substitute teacher had no knowledge of the plans for the social science program, it was found that some of the experiences she offered could be used to further the goals of the study. On her first day with the class, the substitute teacher brought to class some things she had collected on a visit to India. As she showed these to the children, she located India on a world map which had been provided for experiences planned for a later date. Up to this point, only a map of the New York City area had been used. The world map was to be used later to further the children's ability to interpret maps and practice their map skills.

The substitute teacher's use of the world map suggested other uses. Several of the children in the class had traveled to distant places. It was decided that the world map would be more meaningful and personal to them if they could mark on the map the cities where they had visited or resided. These included many sections of the United States as well as cities in Europe, the Near East, and Africa. Most of the areas, however, clustered around New York City. The world map was posted on the bulletin board, with pins marking the places of children's visitations and former homes. On several occasions the children returned to the map and used it in a variety of ways. A number of the children showed it to their parents at the opening or closing of the school day. One day a child brought a bamboo bucket to school which had been made in Puerto Rico, and the teacher noted its place of origin on the map. At another time, a child brought a coin bank shaped like a globe, to "share" with the class. This provided the teacher with an opportunity to compare maps and globes, to discuss with the children how they are alike and how they differ. When the children were asked why maps are used when a globe is more like the earth, one child replied, "The wall is flat and you can't put a globe on it because the wall isn't round. So they make it (the map) flat."

While this is not an accurate answer to the question it demonstrates a beginning grasp of the function of the flat maps. Such a map is used to represent areas of the earth which need to be shown on a scale and in detail not possible on a globe.

Another source of relevant but unplanned experiences was the Civil War Centennial which occurred at this time. Several neighborhood bookstores had special displays in their windows to celebrate the anniversary. There were also special shows on television which some of the children watched. Once a child brought to class a facsimile map from the Civil War era. This was shown to the class and provided another opportunity to note different kinds of maps. Sparked by this idea, a few children on occasion drew free-form "maps" of various places during the work period. One child brought to school a doll that was dressed as a Confederate soldier.

> "A Confederate soldier," said Lois, showing the doll.
> "Why did your mother send it?" asked the teacher.
> "My friend is a Confederate," Lois replied.
> "Where is your friend?"
> "In Tuscumbia," Lois said.
> "Is that in Alabama?"
> "I don't know," Lois said.
> "Has anyone heard of the Civil War?"
> "A long time ago," said Randy, "when it was the Civil War, a lot of people got dead."
> "My father was in the war," Jack volunteered.
> "We're going to cut out pictures from the newspaper about the Civil War," was Randy's last comment.

The children knew that the Civil War was a "long time ago" but they could not distinguish the Civil War from the war in which Jack's father served. The next day, another child brought to class some pictures from a magazine about the Civil War.

> "I brought some pictures of the Civil War and my mother cut them out of *Life* Magazine. This is a man who collected things from the Civil War," said Randy, showing his picture to the class. "This is the North flag and the East flag."
> The teacher asked why the war was fought.
> "The East . . . West," said Randy.
> The teacher quickly put in, "South."
> ". . . wanted to have their own country," Randy went on. "Inside they are shooting out cannons. And the North won."

"Did they have airplanes a hundred years ago?" asked the teacher.

"Yes," some of the children replied.

"How long is a hundred years?"

"A long time ago," several children said.

"The Civil War was still on nights," put in Sally.

"Sometimes brothers fight brothers," said Saul.

The teacher showed the children some old newspapers and pictures of the Civil War era.

Randy said, "Sometimes wars are across oceans and they don't have to fight."

Another child said, pointing to a picture, "Look, there's Abraham Lincoln."

"Was he in the Civil War?" the teacher asked.

"No," said one child.

"Maybe he was a general," said another child.

But Saul said, "Abraham Lincoln was the president before George Washington."

"No," Sally corrected. "He was after."

The teacher was unable to pursue this discussion because of other commitments. On the following day she found an opportunity to reopen the subject in order to help the children clarify some of the historical ideas they had been grappling with the preceding day. She reminded the children of the window display in a local bookstore about the Civil War:

"Yesterday we were talking about pictures," the teacher began. "We saw some pictures about the Civil War. Did anybody see any other pictures of the Civil War?"

"I saw the bookstore," said Saul, referring to the window display. "I saw troopers. I saw a cannon about this big. I saw about twelve men. They were lined up. They had a bomb in the back. It backfired and hit one of their men."

"Did anyone see anything on television?"

"Yesterday I saw a picture of a cannon," Randy said.

"Was it used in the Civil War?"

Randy nodded. "And pistols and rifles. In the old days they had pistols, not guns."

"Did anyone find out what the Civil War was about?" asked the teacher.

"Slaves," said Sally. "They wanted to keep them."

"Which side wanted to keep them?"

"The South," said Randy.

"Which section do we live in?" asked the teacher.
"New York," supplied another child.

Although the answer the teacher hoped to elicit was "the North," she knew that there are always loose ends in children's thinking and that, after further experiences, the children would begin to place New York within the larger geographical context of "the North."

This discussion helped the children to make sense out of some of the information they had been collecting. These children were able to state two important reasons for the Civil War: secession and slavery. Despite the children's lack of understanding of the ramifications of the complex series of events leading to the Civil War, they were able to construct initial understandings about a long-ago period upon which clearer and more detailed understandings could be built. The discussions cited above indicate some of the wide range of information children collect from the many sources available to them and the kinds of confusions likely to result when children try to make sense and order out of masses of information.

The evidence indicated that children can not help collecting historical information from many sources today. The teacher can choose either to ignore this information or to try to find some fruitful ways to help children overcome confusion and begin to clarify the meanings and relationships which they will eventually have to grasp. The second alternative was the one which this study explored. The results appeared to confirm its value, despite the difficulty young children have in visualizing chronological time. The study indicated that five-year-olds could make gross distinctions between long-ago and now. This distinction seems basic to the finer, chronological distinctions that children learn to make with considerably more experience.

The Neighborhood as a Laboratory

When Lucy Sprague Mitchell took young children into the neighborhood to observe and interpret social science data, she wanted children to have the most direct and concrete contact that she could provide with manifestations of significant ideas. In the development of the geographic concepts of this study, it became apparent that work on the harbor might need to give way to work on an area which could be experienced even closer to the children's lives. It was difficult, for example, to continue with a study of the harbor until children had a better grasp of certain ideas about maps. These ideas could be more readily achieved by using the immediate community around the school. Therefore, it was decided to leave the study of the harbor for awhile in order to concentrate on developing some specific basic understandings which could be related to concepts about the harbor later.

An important problem in mapping, for example, which the children had not been able to solve, was that of perspective. They had not understood that a map represents an area as though it is seen from directly above. They needed some vivid experience to make clear the meaning of perspective. To help them develop this idea, they were taken to the top of a very tall building in the neighborhood to look down upon the local area. They saw familiar objects from an unfamiliar vantage point. It was hoped that this experience with perspective would be transferred to the child's understanding of maps and aerial photographs. Slides of the neighborhood as seen from above were taken on this trip to be used later.

A teacher-made map of the neighborhood was used in the classroom when the children returned from their trip to the tall building. In the ensuing discussion, the lines and spaces on the map were related to the streets they knew and to the way the streets looked from above. This map was a frequent source of reference when the class undertook a series of short walks through the neighborhood. Walking along different streets and relating these streets to lines on the map helped the children understand the concepts of distance and direction, both in reality and on a map. The children began to apply their growing knowledge, referring to such directional terms as north and south, instead of uptown and downtown.

The children were encouraged to play out their growing understanding in the block area. Long strips of shelving paper were taped to the floor to represent streets and the streets were labeled, to help with orientation. Children built along these streets structures with which they were familiar, being careful to place buildings on the correct streets. Walking around these block structures, the children oriented themselves within this neighborhood representation, relating directions in the block structure to directions in reality.

This apparent tangent from the goals of the study was not a departure in fact. It constituted a clearer way to present perspective and distance within the immediate neighborhood in order to conceptualize perspective and distance within the larger geographic area of the New York City harbor.

Applying Concepts Developed in the Neighborhood

The program returned to the topic of New York as a harbor after this brief sojourn in the immediate neighborhood. The children were now better able to understand some geographic concepts and representations. At this point, several opportunities were offered to help the children apply some of their developing understandings to the topic of the harbor.

A three-dimensional map of the New York City area made by the researcher was introduced for children's study, manipulation, and play. The land areas were at a higher level than the water areas on this map. Further differentiation between land and water was achieved through the use of color and texture. Some of the children readily recognized the three-dimensional map as a map of the New York area, as indicated by the following discussion:

> The researcher asked the children if they knew what it was.
> "It's a map of the world," Harold said.
> "It's a map of the United States harbor," Saul corrected him.
> "It's the New York harbor," Randy volunteered.
> The researcher pointed to Manhattan Island on the map and asked, "Who knows what this is?"
> Again it was Randy who answered, "Manhattan Island."
> Pointing to the blue area on the map, the researcher asked, "What's this?"
> Several children replied together, "Hudson River."
> The children then went on to identify Staten Island and Long Island on the map. The researcher stuck pins on the map to identify the location of the school and of the ferry depots in Manhattan and Staten Island which the children remembered from their ferry boat ride. The following week Edward remembered which pin on the map indicated the school's location.

Marking on the map the location of geographical places which the children visited or which they knew well, such as ferry depots, the school, and routes taken on trips, helped the children to see the relationship of the map to the physical reality it represented. Using toy boats and cars, the children played with this map, dramatizing their growing understandings just as they had done earlier with blocks.

At the beginning of the study, children's conceptions of maps were rather limited to the understanding that there are road maps which "show where you're supposed to go." They did not understand that there are different kinds of maps which are used for different purposes. They had practically no understanding of cardinal direction, perspective, and scale. The study helped the children to grasp some understanding of the variety of types of maps and purposes for which maps are used. Some progress was also made in scale, perspective, and cardinal direction, although these concepts are of sufficient complexity to require considerably more study and experience.

Various review activities helped children to recall, to categorize, and to analyze their earlier activities. Viewing slides which had been taken during the study on various trips was a striking aid to recollection and analysis. Further discussion also provided clarification, detail, and meaning. Once again the children were asked to draw a floor plan of their classroom. The results were much the same as in their first attempt, indicating much greater increase in understanding of representation through block construction than through drawing of floor plans. These results might have been anticipated in a program which neither offered children direction in drawing nor made any requirements of them in this respect. The children's growing ability to represent some areas of physical reality in block constructions suggested that this is a much more productive activity for five-year-olds than drawing, which requires much more experience and practice.

One reason for the selection of the topic of the New York harbor for this study was that it offered the possibility of testing young children's ability to surmount the well-entrenched "here-and-now" barrier which has been imposed for so long upon the kindergarten curriculum. It was planned to test and explore some ways of helping children to gain some understanding about places outside of their immediate environment and about events which had occurred in the past. The relationship of the harbor to the whole wide world outside through trade and travel could interest children in learning about the remote in space. Studying physical and cultural changes in the harbor in the past could lead to learning about the remote in time. The topic of the harbor, therefore, seemed to offer an excellent opportunity to evaluate the possibility that young children could begin to develop some conceptions of the far-away and the long-ago.

DEALING WITH THE LONG-AGO

Two important aspects of history were included in this program. It was planned to see if children could begin to grasp a sense of the long-ago and its relationship to the present and the concepts of historical time and chronology. The study of the harbor offered a variety of ways of dealing with these concepts. The children were familiar with some ideas about the Hudson River since it flowed near their homes. This familiarity was used to help children move as far back in time as the discovery of the Hudson River. Pictures, models, and other representations of the city and of ships helped to bring the past nearer to these children. Trips around the city and the visit to the Museum of the City of New York also helped the children tie some ideas about the past to the present.

The study of historical concepts began during the second period of the program. The class had walked a few blocks to observe the boats on the river. The children had looked at maps of the Port of New York and had identified the river on these maps. During a discussion period, the children were told the story of Henry Hudson and his voyage of discovery. The discussion included the meaning of the concept of discovery in this context. One child interpreted the story to mean, "He found the river." During this discussion a picture of the *Half-Moon* was shown to the children, and they were told that this was the boat Henry Hudson had used in his explorations. The children talked about the way this boat looked and how it differed from modern boats.

The children knew immediately that that boat was from the "olden days." One child thought it was the *Mayflower*, but he was challenged by another who contended that, if it were the *Mayflower*, "it would have a flower on it." Another child thought it was a pirate ship. These comments indicated that the children could identify a boat as being from a previous era even though their knowledge of history was scanty. They could not relate ships either to a particular era or event in history but they knew these were old-fashioned in some way. This understanding represents a beginning step toward a grasp of the significance of change which has taken place through time.

Since there was limited interest in this thread of the program, it was cut short at this point. It was hoped that the children's ideas about the past which were developing could be used at a later stage. The next endeavor was an attempt to help the children develop a concept of chronological time through a concrete representation of time.

The Time-Line

Several days after the discussion about Henry Hudson, a rope was brought into the classroom. This rope was marked off in one-foot sections, each section representing one year. The entire rope was five and one-half feet long, representing the average age of the children in the kindergarten. There was a discussion and explanation of the rope. A story of a child's development, from birth through his entrance into kindergarten, was related to the class with the appropriate portion of the rope used to signify each age. Different parts of the line were then designated and the children were asked to state the age of the child represented at each period. The children responded appropriately from "no age" through the kindergarten period. When asked if this line could represent the teacher, the children responded negatively, stating that such a line would have to be "Ohhh . . . really long." The responses showed that the children understood the periods of time used here and could relate the representation to the passage of time appropriately.

Several weeks later, this type of representation was resumed. On this occasion the rope used was as long as the room itself. This rope represented three hundred and fifty years, the range of history from the discovery of the Hudson River to the present. This time-line was compared with the one previously used, in relation to both the period of time covered and actual size. Since the children had learned much about ships through this program, each era on the line was marked with an appropriate ship, starting with the *Half-Moon* on one end, ranging through square riggers, clipper ships, and early steamers and ending with a modern ocean liner on the other end. The assumption was that the children's familiarity with boats, both modern and old-fashioned, would help them to place the various times represented on the line.

The children, however, were only able to make the rough differentiation between modern ships and ships of the past. They could not differentiate between the more recent and the more remote past either in regard to ships or the representation of time. The finer differentiation would obviously have to develop more gradually, over a longer period of time.

Visiting the Museum

One of the experiences in the study which was most successful in bringing a sense of reality to the past was a visit to the Museum of the City of New York. Here the children had many clues to the city as it was long ago. Pictures, collections of realia, and dioramas of familiar places as they were in the past all made information about the past more vivid and concrete to the children. It helped them to learn about the long-ago and to ask questions about those elements that did not fit into their framework of reality.

In the center of one room in the museum was a horse-drawn streetcar. Viewing this, the children compared this public conveyance with the more familiar modern bus, as follows:

"They used to use it," said Lucy, pointing to the streetcar.
"Where did the car go?" asked the teacher.
"It carried lots of people," said John.
"Do we use them now?" the teacher asked.
"No," several children replied.
"It was pulled by horses," remarked one child.
"Why did they need horses if they were on railroad tracks?" asked Marc.
"There were no engines, so they needed horses," the teacher replied.

A little later, Harold was heard to remark, "This is a trolley car on tracks. The wagon trains out west have no tracks."

This trip to the museum made a strong impact on the children's thinking. The opportunity to view evidence of the past in vivid representations seemed to give all the children a feeling for historical time. Their attitude was best summarized by one child who, standing in front of a diorama of Bowling Green as it looked in the nineteenth century, exclaimed, "If I didn't see it, I wouldn't have believed it."

The children made many references to the museum trip in school. Several children built a museum out of unit blocks in the classroom. They used this structure to recall and describe quite adequately the objects they had seen in various parts of the museum.

DEALING WITH THE
REMOTE IN SPACE

Although the program concentrated primarily on the local harbor, the nature of the topic seemed to lead the children to the far-away. The destination and points of origin of ocean-going vessels necessarily pointed to remote geographical areas, in addition to the international relationships involved in cargo and passenger traffic.

There were many situations in which children were dealing with ideas about remote regions. Some of these are described in the section on map concepts. The experiences with the world map, the inclusion of objects from India in the classroom, children's showing of articles from remote areas, all attest to the kindergarten child's interest in distant places and his ability to deal with the far-away on his own level. The program supported this interest and ability in many ways. Children's play with maps, toy boats and cars, and a ship's wheel were stimuli for thinking about remote places. When children played they were on boats, they referred to such places as Israel, Africa, Russia, and Japan. The children knew that Africa is across the ocean and that Israel is far away. During play, one child stated, "In Africa the people never saw New York."

The children's discussions about far-off places indicated many misconceptions and stereotyped thoughts. When a visitor from India was introduced to a child he responded to the query, "Do you know where that is?" with "Yeah, it's far away in the Wild West where the cowboys live." Africa was usually referred to within the context of big-game hunting, and Japan became the focus of dramatic play whose content consisted of children's flying toy airplanes over a block city, shouting, "Bombs over Tokyo! Bombs over Tokyo!" In each of these cases it seemed that the children were associating geographic place-names with the content of television programs and, especially, reruns of old movies. One of the desirable goals of this program might be to balance the picture children receive about distant places from the mass media with a more realistic and understandable view of the world.

REVIEW OF
THE PROGRAM

This study clearly indicates the many ways in which today's five-year-olds collect information of historical and geographic nature. Personal experience, television, and other mass media are making children aware of people and places remote in time and space. Kindergarten children are seen as trying to understand their own world in their attempts to make sense out of the masses of information they receive. They are also seen to be living in a world whose here-and-now includes more distant geographic areas than ever before and whose present moment is bombarded with ideas and information relating to the past as well as to the future. Children of change today can no longer be unaware of historical change even though understanding of more detailed chronological change must come more slowly with further experience.

Various aspects of the program described above were presented in parallel during the study. Each aspect represented a single thread that was being woven into the cloth of the social studies curriculum in this kindergarten class. Many other threads could similarly be isolated and described. All these threads would eventually be structured by the children, it was thought, into distinct textures and patterns, although many loose threads would be apparent at the early stage of conceptualization. This idea of concepts-in-formation over long periods of time was illustrated many times during the study.

Throughout the study, there was a continual need to develop activities in which children could be active participants, rather than passive receptors. Experiences also had to be shaped to the children's level of understanding, to help them achieve the ideas and concepts which had been defined in the goals of the program. The teacher needed to evaluate the success of the planned activities regularly. New activities had to be added when it was apparent that the children had not grasped the ideas presented. When concepts of perspective and direction did not emerge from a study of the New York harbor, it seemed necessary to study the neighborhood which was closer to the children's lives and where new ideas could be better understood. This interaction of innovation and evaluation extended throughout the program. The concepts identified as the goals provided the criteria by which to determine the success of the program. Were these concepts becoming understandable to the children? If not, how else could the concepts be presented or represented? These concepts became powerful tools for curriculum development, which could be used in a variety of other programs.

BIBLIOGRAPHY

California State Department of Education, *Building a Curriculum in the Social Studies*, Sacramento: Author, 1957.

Johnson, Henry, *Teaching of History*, New York: Macmillan, 1940.

Mitchell, Lucy Sprague, *Here and Now Storybook*, New York: E. P. Dutton, 1921.

———, *Young Geographers*, New York: John Day, 1934.

National Council for the Social Studies, Committee on Concepts and Values, *A Guide to Content in the Social Studies*, Washington, D.C.: National Council for the Social Studies, 1958.

Pratt, Caroline, *Experimental Practices in City and Country School*, New York: E. P. Dutton, 1924.

Quillan, James J., and Lavone A. Hanna, *Education for Social Competency*, Chicago: Scott, Foresman, 1961.

Preston, James (Ed.), *New Viewpoints in Geography*, Twenty-ninth Yearbook, Washington, D.C.: National Council for the Social Studies, 1959.

Spodek, Bernard, "Developing Social Science Concepts in the Kindergarten," unpublished Ed.D. Project, Teachers College, Columbia University, 1962.

3

LEARNING ECONOMIC
CONCEPTS IN THE
KINDERGARTEN

Economic concepts are more closely related to young children's lives than is generally realized. Their experiences in accompanying parents on marketing and shopping trips, making small purchases of their own, becoming aware of family occupations, of budget problems, and of advertising, through television and other media, provide five-year-olds with a surprising volume of prior experiences and encounters with economic phenomena. The young child, however, usually has fragmentary impressions of his experiences, and he is more likely to notice the "magic-eye" door of the supermarket than the money exchange at the cash register. Thus the child has many perceptions and impressions which convey little meaning to him because he lacks a framework of understanding from which to view his experiences. He sees many people in a store, but he has no conception of the relationships between buyer and seller or customer and store worker, and therefore no basis for differentiation is apparent to him.

The young child has experiences in economic transactions for which he has no guides to meaning; in addition, he has a life-long need to be an intelligent citizen in economic affairs for the benefit of his own family and that of the community. Therefore, the rationale for selection of economic concepts to test in a kindergarten study rests on the child's learning needs—both present and future.

SOURCES OF
ECONOMIC CONCEPTS

To construct the first rung of a ladder of understanding between the large abstractions of economics and the chance impressions of five-year-olds required considerable planning. The effort to explore the teaching of beginning economic concepts began with a selection of a few key economic concepts to be studied.

When this study began, a group of economists and educators had just completed a report which defined the basic economic concepts to be taught in high schools, and this report became the basis for the study of economic concepts in the kindergarten. Three key concepts were selected from the report of the National Task Force on Economic Education.[1] These were:

1. *Economic interdependence*—the central role of the price and market system in a money economy. It is the need to pay a price that shuts some consumers out of the market at any time. If the commodity is in short supply relative to the demand the price will be bid up and more consumers will be shut out. If producing more of a commodity results in lowering the cost, this will tend to increase the amount supplied and will lower the price and permit more consumers to buy the product. Thus price is the regulator in a private-enterprise market type economy.

2. *Scarcity*—the economic factor of scarcity and the need for economizing resources. This same concept is applicable at the household level.

3. *Economic production*—the process of converting resources into goods and services to satisfy human wants. The process of production includes both the output of goods and services.

These three key concepts were elaborated into a statement of understandings of these ideas appropriate to five-year-olds, in terms of the topic selected for study, New York's Food Supply, essentially as follows:

A. Food supply and economic interdependence.
  1. All the people who live in New York City need food but there is no room to grow food here.
  2. All the food for the people in the city must come from farms

[1] Report of the National Task Force on Economic Education, *Economic Education in the Schools*, New York: Committee for Economic Development, 1961, pp. 23–28.

outside the city. The food is brought in by different kinds of transportation from many places.

3. All families in New York City are consumers.
4. Families buy food in different kinds of stores. These stores must have food delivered to them almost every day.
5. Each food product has a price. Some prices change often while some seldom change.
6. Store managers fill their stores with things they think people will buy. Each family looks at prices to decide what foods to buy.
7. Families earn money for work and use this money to buy food.
8. There are many supermarkets in New York, where different foods are kept in different places.
9. Big trucks deliver food to the supermarket. Machines are used to unload the trucks.

B. Producers.
1. Everybody who works to earn money is a producer. Producers may produce goods or services.
2. Farmers who grow food produce goods; people who sell food in stores produce services.
3. There are many different jobs in supermarkets. These include manager and assistant manager, stock man, truck driver and assistant, produce clerk, butcher and assistant, and checker.

C. Scarcity and the need for economizing.
1. There is not enough of all the foods people might want.
2. Most families do not have as much income as they would like. Some families have more income than others.
3. There are some things that every family must have. These are necessities. The things that families can buy after they buy the things they need are luxuries.
4. Usually the more there is of something, the lower the price. The less there is of something, like steak, the higher the price.

D. Machines and the division of labor.
1. Most goods are made in large factories where many people work and where machines are used.
2. Some machines are small and simple and others are large and complicated.
3. Machines help people because they can make things better, faster and cheaper. Some things cannot be made without machines.

These ideas were spelled out in simple terms, not because they were to be taught to the children, but because experiences and materials had to be chosen and shaped to yield some of these understandings. After the selected ideas were simply stated, ways of developing some of the essential attributes of these concepts became apparent and it was possible to list some specific materials and learning experiences to be introduced.[2]

The method of an "emerging" curriculum was specifically rejected in favor of a deliberate choice of ideas, materials, and experiences. However, children vary infinitely and no two classes ever duplicate each other in prior experiences, information, or understandings. Therefore, it was felt that even a highly planned program must have sufficient elements of open-endedness, flexibility, and adaptability so that a body of ideas can become meaningful to a designated group of children. This point of view required weekly, and sometimes daily, evaluations of the children's progress toward the selected concepts, with changes or modifications of the program or of improvisation when this seemed necessary.

New York's Food Supply was chosen as the topic for the study after consultation with the classroom teacher. This topic was not the only possible choice. The three key concepts selected, *economic interdependence*, *scarcity*, and *economic production*, could have emerged from studies of farming in a rural school district, of factory production in industrial towns or cities, of transportation in almost any community or even of the traditional study of community helpers. The teacher's own family background in a store contributed many details, insights, and suggestions for program which added much to the study. Teachers who have strength in particular areas do well to capitalize these assets in their teaching, as this classroom teacher chose to do.

PREPLANNING

The study began, then, with a listing of the ideas to be developed, plus a topic chosen to be the vehicle of the study. A group of experiences was preplanned which seemed to offer good possibilities both for children's self-propelled play and for teacher guidance toward selected concepts. It was agreed that the primary in-class experience would be a store-play project which the children would be encour-

[2] Helen F. Robison, "Learning Economic Concepts in the Kindergarten," unpublished Ed.D. Project, Teachers College, Columbia University, 1963.

aged to develop. Store play was to be supported throughout the study by the addition from time to time of props and by related experiences to revive flagging interest, as well as to add information and help to illuminate some of the concepts under study. The specific props to be introduced into store play over a period of time were also preselected, as well as some movies, books, games, scrapbooks, and a few, but not all, of the supporting and related experiences.

During the study, the researcher had weekly conferences with the classroom teacher, usually at lunchtime, to evaluate the group's concept development, recalling and analyzing children's activities and verbalizations. These conferences usually resulted in further planning for additional ways to guide the children's play or for additional experiences or materials to be explored, when further progress seemed to require this. Plans were always subject to change or modification, depending upon the children's reactions or other requirements of the class.

The study of economic concepts became one of the many ongoing activities in the classroom. On a few occasions an activity was scheduled which overshadowed all other classroom centers of interest, as when a class trip was taken to the supermarket or when cookies were baked and sold. But these were rare events, and, for the most part, the study of economic concepts was pursued along with a multitude of other ideas and energetic activities.

Preplanned experiences for the study of economic concepts included the following:

1. A store play project, with its props.
2. Work on the concept of families, using blocks, construction paper figures, a flannel board and flannel blocks and figures, and a bar graph.
3. One trip to the supermarket.
4. A cookie-baking experience and a cookie sale.
5. A project to demonstrate division of labor, making paper flower-baskets.
6. Reading selected books and stories.
7. Showing educational films.
8. Use of a simple 8-millimeter projector by children, showing two specially prepared movies about the supermarket.
9. Use of an opaque projector with pictures clipped from magazines.
10. A visit to the classroom by a supermarket manager.

It was hoped that many of the children would become interested in store play and would continue to play store roles in increasingly distinctive and knowledgeable ways. It was expected that such free dramatic play would contribute to children's increasing awareness of the details of economic transactions in stores and of relationships involved. As more information became available to children and as guided discussions helped them to understand some concepts more clearly, it was expected that the children's spontaneous dramatic play in the store would reflect this growing understanding in sharper differentiation of store roles and more knowledgeable detail in the use of the store props. The teacher's periodic observation of this play and her daily discussions with the children were seen as informal evaluative techniques. Listening to the store play conversation and noting its development revealed the level of children's understandings and indicated their confusions and misunderstandings. At "evaluation time," at the end of the free play or work period, children's descriptions and discussions of their play furnished a further opportunity to assess their conceptual progress. In addition, this daily discussion offered the teacher regular opportunities to offer information or clarification to which the children appeared to be receptive. Weekly planning conferences between the teacher and the researcher assessed the process of conceptual growth and resulted in specific plans for further day-to-day programming.

To open the study of food stores, a book was read to the class, *Big Store, Funny Door,*[3] which featured the "electric eye" door with which most of the children were already familiar. It also served to initiate a discussion about supermarkets and food marketing. The next day, a letter, which had been written on a primer typewriter, was read and distributed to the children to take home. The letter requested the parents to take the children along on the next family marketing trip to observe the variety of foods in the store and the different jobs people did in the store. From the beginning children's

---

[3] Betty Russell, *Big Store, Funny Door,* Chicago: Albert Whitman and Company, 1955.

attention was directed to selective observation and to detailed information needed for generalization and categorization.

During the following week, while various children began to report they had gone marketing and there was mounting impatience to share information, the concept of the family was introduced, together with representational and symbolic modes of presenting numerical data. Since the work on the concept of families was repeated toward the end of the study, it will be described later.

About one week later, a lively class discussion permitted the children to report and share their observations in the food stores. Experience charts were constructed from the many details the children supplied. Some children volunteered to dictate stories about their marketing experiences and some factual, as well as fanciful, stories resulted. Several picture scrapbooks were added to the library corner but were seldom used.[4] The next day, the teacher read a story about marketing, stimulating another group discussion which tapped more of the store information in the class and permitted further sharing and exchange of ideas.[5]

At this point, it was thought store play could be introduced. A small-scale room divider with a suggestion of a store counter was borrowed from another classroom and placed in the block corner one day when several boys were working in this area.

> "What is it?" asked Henry.
> "What do you think it could be?" the researcher asked.
> "It could be a house," he suggested.
> "Yes, it could," agreed the researcher.
> He stood behind it, framed by the counter and top shelf, and grinned. "It could be a supermarket," he said.
> "Let's play blocks!" demanded Jimmy impatiently, pulling Henry back to block play. They both turned their backs on the room divider.
> Since the block corner looked unpromising, the room divider was moved over next to the housekeeping corner and some empty food cartons were taken from the housekeeping corner refrigerator and placed on the counter. Jane and Mona decided to play store and both stood behind the counter. Mona meowed and the researcher asked Jane if Mona were a cat. Jane nodded and pretended to pour milk

---

[4] The teacher suggested that, because these children were generally well-supplied with books at home, with parents eager to read to them, they perhaps had less interest in browsing through books in school than in social interaction.

[5] *First Stories To Read Aloud*, New York: Wonder Books, 1959, pp. 131–136.

from an empty carton into a dish and put the dish on the floor. Mona, meowing and crawling, pretended to drink milk.

Phoebe approached the counter to see what was happening and the researcher suggested that she might want to buy something and she said she did. The researcher suggested that she get some paper to cut up to use as money and she did.

Pat, noting that store play was in progress, went to the far corner of the room, returning with the toy cash register, which he deposited on the counter. Meanwhile, Phoebe returned with some cut-up newspaper and the researcher suggested that she use this as money to make some purchases.

Thus, store play was initiated with some stage setting, verbal encouragement and suggestions from the researcher. From then on, until well after the end of the study, the store activities were carried on daily by varying groups of children at different times and with much variation in performance. Store play became such a popular activity in the class that it soon became the regular activity of the early arrivals. While waiting for the opening formalities, groups of children just naturally concentrated in the store, arranging "stock" or "buying" and "selling."

Once launched, the store play was encouraged by the occasional addition of simple props, to provide novelty and interest, to suggest different dimensions of play, to encourage different children to pursue various forms of play, and to maintain children's interest in the play long enough for concepts to develop. The children frequently saved food containers and brought them to school so that the store "stock" grew steadily. Other props included:

1. A large number and variety of empty food cartons and cans.
2. Large cardboard cartons, used as shelves in the store.
3. Pictures of food which were placed on the wall in the back of the store area.
4. Several dozen double-handled shopping bags.
5. A supply of cash register tapes saved from food purchases.
6. Play money.
7. Advertising posters about food "specials," secured from advertising agencies.
8. Paper signs indicating food prices, made by children.
9. A metal coin changer.
10. Pocketbooks and additional toy money.
11. Plastic toy telephones with dials and bells.
12. Paper and pencils for writing, as needed.

13. Once, small boxes of real raisins were deposited in the store, resulting in a fast sell-out.

The metal coin changer, for example, which was not strictly needed for store play, appealed to some boys who were not interested in other aspects of store play. They were delighted to strap the coin changer to their belts and to help make change, or play bus driver, or just enjoy manipulating the play coins. The provision of several telephones, instead of only one, encouraged communication between the store and the housekeeping area, permitting many children to become involved in some aspects of the buying and selling.

Had it been possible to provide several other props, as a shopping cart and a scale to weigh "produce," which had been planned but had not been provided in time, additional play and manipulative activities would have been available to more children and would have interested some children who were less involved in store transactions. When the girls who regularly inhabited the housekeeping area unexpectedly found several pocketbooks bulging with fresh toy money one day, buying groceries resumed some of the popularity which it had lost to other experiences for several days. In this way, fresh stimulation was supplied as needed. Movies, stories, and other media provided additional information which always inspired more interesting play.

USE OF MOVIES

Two brief movies were prepared for the study, to focus the children's attention on selected aspects of supermarket operation. The first one showed the various supermarket workers at their jobs, including the manager, the assistant manager, produce men, stock men, butchers, and checkers. This movie focused on the concept of the variety of jobs in the supermarket or the specialization of functions which make possible the retail food service. The second movie focused on the delivery of foods to the store, showing the trucks, the unloading operations and methods of bringing food into the store. This movie concerned not only the transportation required to bring food to urban families but, of course, led to the concept of interdependence, that is, that city families depend on out-of-city food growers and transporters for their food supply.

These movies were not only distinguished for their brevity and sharp focus, but also for the manipulative experience they provided to the children. A simple 8mm projector was made available for the children to operate themselves. This is practically an automatic projector, with the film encased in a self-loading plastic cartridge, permitting the film to be shown continuously until the projector's "off" button is turned. The only controls, which the children quickly mastered, are the focus and the on-and-off button, in addition to the electric plug.

There was great excitement when the children first took turns working the projector. These were silent films so that their showing stimulated much chatter and casual conversation about the contents.[6] An argument developed over whether the butcher was using a knife to cut meat. It was natural to continue running the film until the butcher's sequence showed up again, when it was perceived that it was not a knife but a meat-cutting machine that was being used. In this way, all kinds of detail not noticed at first showing could be studied in subsequent viewings. This made it possible to refer to the movie as to a book, which is available not only on first reading but at subsequent times. On two occasions, when the children were offered further opportunities to operate the projector to view these same two films, there continued to be high interest, although some children were satisfied sooner than others in the number of turns they wanted. More brief movies of this type could have been used to help clarify other ideas included in the study.

Two other educational films were shown to the class, one entitled, "Where Does Our Food Come From?" the other, "How Machines and Tools Help Us."[7] Each film was shown twice, at the children's request, provoking much discussion and noting of detail. Probably, the children would have learned even more from these excellent films could they have been kept for several additional showings. The need for repetition in encounters with new ideas and materials is seldom fully met in kindergarten programs, even when this need is well understood. Even very bright children need leisurely experiencing,

---

[6] However, sound can readily be added to these films, if desired.

[7] "How Machines and Tools Help Us" and "Where Does Our Food Come From?" Chicago: Coronet Films (one reel, color with sound, 11 minutes running time).

observing, and perceiving with opportunities to repeat activities, and slower children require much more repetition before understandings are truly their own.

DEVELOPING
CONCEPTS OF JOBS

At the beginning of the study when the children described their observations in the supermarket, after marketing with their families, they enumerated the following jobs:

"A man was working at the scale, weighing food, especially fruits and vegetables."
"A man was at the cash register, checking food."
"A man was bringing food into the store."
"A man was putting prices on food, using a stamp."
"A man was putting food on shelves."
"A man was using a machine to slice bread."
"A man was using a meat-cutting machine."

Despite this clear listing of store occupations, most children played one of two roles in store play, that of either storekeeper or customer. This may have been because the physical area allotted to store play was small and confining, more suggestive of a small grocery store than a supermarket. Whenever the opportunity offered, the possibility of job differentiation was suggested or it was pointedly noted when it occurred. The movie on supermarket jobs helped to make these job distinctions more vivid and understandable. However, some children confused terms when describing their play, and other children were unable to make some of the simple distinctions at first. As these confusions became apparent, the teacher began to ask more and more searching questions at evaluation time, to clarify misunderstandings, as follows:

On March 19, at evaluation time, Steve said he had played in the store.
"Were you a customer or the storekeeper?" asked the teacher.
"A customer."
"What did you buy?"
"Oh," said Steve, "I was the storekeeper."
"Who were your customers?"
Steve named several children.

Phoebe said she had played in the store, too.
"What did you buy?"
"Crackers and milk," said Phoebe.
"What did you do with the food?"
"I ate it."

Over a period of time, it was gradually established that a customer bought food for her own consumption while a storekeeper sold food to customers. This distinction was not as obvious to five-year-olds as most adults would assume. Further distinctions were made about three weeks later, when Steve described his store play by saying, "First I was a customer, then a storekeeper, then a delivery boy." As a storekeeper, he said, "I put things on shelves, and I took money."

Here Harold objected. "The boss in the store tells people what to do," he said, scornfully. "He doesn't do things, he doesn't sell things and put things on shelves. There are seven or eight people who take money for food. There are long lines of customers."

The teacher seized on Harold's account of job differentiation in the supermarket and asked, "What do you call the people who put food on shelves?"

"Producers," said Steve, because this term had been introduced several times before.

"All the people who work in stores are producers," the researcher interrupted. "Producers are workers. The man who puts food on shelves is called a stock clerk. There is a lot of work for the stock men."

The teacher added, "That's what you were doing, Steve. You were a stock clerk."

"I was a customer," put in Betsy. "I bought eggs and all the groceries for the week."

When the class walked to a nearby supermarket to buy groceries, the focus was primarily on the ingredients needed to bake cookies, but the children were again asked to notice different kinds of jobs people were doing in the store. The class discussion after the trip indicated further progress in job concepts:

"I saw a man cutting boxes open," one child said.
"I saw a man stamping prices," said another.
"I saw a woman getting milk," said one child.
"Was she a worker in the store?" asked the researcher.

"No!" chorused the group, and several added, "She was a customer."

"What were we today when we were buying food in the store?" the researcher asked.

"We were customers," said Sheila.

"What are customers?" said the researcher.

"People who buy things. Persons who buy things," Sheila replied thoughtfully and precisely.

"Does anyone know any other name for customers?" There was no reply. "Consumers. Customers are also consumers. We were consumers," said the researcher.

Some further job differentiation began to occur in store play soon after this.

Steve said, "I played in the store and Marty was the delivery boy and he delivered stuff to Dorothy and Betsy."

"How did you like your job, Marty?" asked the teacher.

"Oh, all right."

"Did you get anything for your work?"

"Yes," said Marty.

"I gave him a paper dollar and a nickel," Steve volunteered.

Another day, David said when he played store, he took the money and Mary added that checkers take money in the supermarket. The next day, Eddie described his store play, explaining that there were two jobs in the store, that of manager and "to put food on shelves."

Since very few children were aware at the beginning of the study that it is the customer who pays the storekeeper or checker, rather than the other way around, much progress had been made in establishing the money transaction as a necessity for purchasing. But Joe continued to be confused about the correct words to describe the different roles. One day, he said he had played store and was a customer. When the teacher asked him what products he had bought, it was revealed that he had not been purchasing but selling food. The study underlined the importance of searching and probing for children's understandings and for refraining from the conclusion that all children share the clearer ideas of the more verbal and experienced children.

Toward the end of the study, after the teacher read the book, *Daddies, What They Do All Day*,[8] the following discussion ensued:

[8] Helen Walker Puner, *Daddies, What They Do All Day*, New York: Lothrop, Lee and Shepard, 1946.

Jimmy said, "Some daddies stay home. They don't want to work. When daddies go on vacation, they don't work."

Dorothy said, "A man in my building doesn't work. He's retired. He's old."

"What other jobs do daddies do?" the researcher asked.

"Work steady," Alice said.

"Daddy who teaches in college," said Henry.

"Garbage men—they take garbage," said Ellen.

"They make money," David contributed.

"Some daddies travel at sea," Pat added.

"Why do daddies work?" the researcher asked.

"To make money," said Pat.

"What other jobs can you think of?"

"Bus driver," said Dorothy.

"Man who works in post office," said Mary.

"Schoolteacher," said Steve.

"Banker," said Mona. "He keeps money."

"Nobody *makes* money," Harold objected, breaking into the conversation. "You get money. The people you work for *give* you money."

"Skin diver," said Sheila. "He might get some fish and bring it home for dinner. Skin diver might get money for what he finds. Skin divers find things."

"Person who drives a taxi," said Ellen.

"Man who works in a store," said Pat. "He could be a grocery man, clerk, manager, storekeeper, salesman."

"Man who directs band—a band director," Sheila said.

"Man who works for jewelry shop. He sells jewelry," said Laura.

"Meat cutter—butcher," said Alice.

"Newspaperman prints newspapers," said Laura.

"Artist," said Sheila.

"People buy their pictures," Jimmy explained. "That's how he makes money."

"He can cook models out of clay," Sheila went on. "Carpenter people make statues. A scientist mixes things and sees what they 'turn out come like'."

"A movie star acts in the movies," Laura said.

"Some mothers have jobs too," the researcher began.

"She can be a nurse," Sheila was quick to volunteer.

"They can do cooking," said Dorothy.

"Some mothers could be dancers," Ellen said.

"Some mothers could clean houses," said Phoebe.

This discussion was remarkable on several counts. All of it is relevant and indicates some understanding of the concept under discussion, fathers' occupations or jobs and, to a lesser extent, mothers' occupations. Fifteen children out of the twenty-one present made contributions to the discussion, which is an unusually high proportion of involvement for five-year-olds. The children could supply so many examples of each category discussed that they were able to toss the discussion from child to child with little intervention from adults. The discussion indicated a rather stable concept of fathers' jobs by most of the children. There was less clarity about mothers' occupations, which were not stressed at all in the study. Cooking and cleaning houses were equated with gainful employment in such jobs as nurse or dancer. Of course, these could be gainfully employed cooks and house-workers but, in consideration of the children's backgrounds and the context in which they used these terms, it is far more likely that they were referring to the duties of their own mothers as housewives at home.

Further light on store jobs was shed by a supermarket manager when he came to visit the class. One of the questions the children had prepared in advance was: What work does the manager do? The manager replied that his job was to see that everyone else did his work properly and that the store made a profit. Other jobs mentioned included the checkers who take money, men who fill shelves so that customers won't find them empty, men who bring food into the store, and men who mark the prices on foods. One child asked whether the manager personally goes to the big market to buy food from the farmers. The manager replied that he could not, since his job was to stay at the store to see that everyone did his work and that nothing was stolen. He said there was a man who bought food for all the stores in this chain of supermarkets and that this was the man who went to the big market.

Sheila asked whether women worked in his store, and, when the manager replied affirmatively, she wanted to know what kinds of jobs they had; he said they were checkers. Margaret told the manager that once, when she was in a supermarket, she saw a store employee count the number of cartons that had just been delivered.

The manager supplied new detail as to store occupations and, since he personified one of them, perhaps helped the children picture his job more specifically and in more personal dimensions. While he also repeated information the children already had, he helped reinforce their understandings, reflecting them clearly and in context and language they could understand and use.

**DEVELOPING CONCEPTS
OF MONEY AND PRICES**

The children in the study developed some significant concepts about money and prices. These included the function and use of cash registers and of cash register tapes, the process by which customers exchange money for goods and the need for making change. They also gained an understanding of denominations of money with some beginning notions of equivalences and gross glimmerings of relative money values, as well as an introduction to the intricacies of the price system. For example, when the children first began to play with the toy cash register, there was much banging with both fists, pushing several keys at once, jamming the cash drawer with paper, pulling the drawer out and letting the contents fall to the floor, and generally manipulating it in a rather random, aimless fashion. Gradually the use of the cash register changed. Sales were rung up by pushing only one or two keys, one at a time, usually after a careful selection of a particular key. The children had begun to notice the number which popped up when they punched a key and they began to read this number through the plastic window. When Pat wanted the customers to know he was closing the store, he would punch the "no sale" key and say testily, "No sale!" Other children copied this and would say, "No sale! Can't you see the store is closed?"

When the toy money became available, the cash drawer began to be opened with great care instead of being purposely or accidentally hurled to the floor. It was worth careful handling to avoid having to scoop up many small coins from the floor and, especially, to prevent other children from "stealing" the store's cash.

Some children began to spend considerable periods of time putting money in the drawer, identifying coins and placing each type of coin in its own compartment. Bills began to be smoothed out and placed in the proper compartment of the cash drawer, instead of being torn and crushed any old way. One day, when Mary had been playing storekeeper, she described her activities at evaluation time as follows:

"At first, I got the money right. It was all mixed up! I put the fifty cents, twenty-five cents in one place, five and tens and pennies in another place. Then they got all mixed up. I got the money out from behind the drawer of the cash register." Billy reported he had helped Mary. Observation records indicated that these two had spent the whole work period "getting the money right."

It was evident that play money had taken on some meaning and that its use in the cash register had changed from manipulative, random play to patterned, meaningful activities, extremely fuzzy as to specific quantitative relationships for some children, but increasingly clear as to its essential function in a money economy—as a medium of exchange.

When it became apparent that many children were unable to identify the various play-money coins, it was decided to play games with groups of about five children involving manipulating and observing the coins. Sometimes, one child was asked to distribute a penny to each of the children at the table from her stock of assorted coins. Or each child was asked to select a coin from a container of assorted coins, identify it, and propose a purchase which could be made with it. In this way, children began to be aware that coins could be identified by the number inscribed on them as well as by comparative size, by color, and in other ways.

The children generally were ignorant of realistic prices, since their experiences in this respect were so limited. The teacher attempted to inject a measure of reality into pricing whenever possible and clarify the process of making change, which caused much confusion.

If a storekeeper asked forty dollars for a can of coffee, the teacher protested it was much too expensive, and when she was charged eight cents for a pint of ice cream, she was very emphatic that it was cheap and she was getting a bargain. When children wanted to write signs advertising food sales, realistic prices were suggested to them for various foods.

In the beginning storekeepers always gave change, if there was any transaction at all. Even when the customer tendered the exact amount, he got change. This was partly due to the sheer fun of manipulation, but, in addition, most children lacked the number concepts required to understand the reason for giving change or the process for computing it. One day, as the concept had been gradually developing that change was not always automatically given, Sheila played customer and gave Elsa money to pay for the groceries. "Don't I get any change?" asked Sheila, as Elsa firmly closed the cash register. "No," said Elsa, positively, "you spent all your money."

> Jimmy, who seemed to understand that the customer does not always receive change, nevertheless liked to make change. When the student teacher ordered some ice cream, he charged her ten cents, accepted her dime, punched the cash register and gave her some change.
> "You don't need to give me change because I gave you the right amount," the student teacher told him.
> "Yes, I do," said Jimmy. "This store is different."
> But later the same morning when the teacher played customer and ordered some juice for which Jimmy charged her eight cents, he gave serious thought to the problem of change. She gave him a dime and requested her change, but he had difficulty figuring the correct amount. He suggested three cents but she told him the correct amount was two cents.

Since the lack of number concepts contributed to the confusion about change, focus on some basic number concepts was indicated but could not be fitted into the schedule. Nevertheless, a cookie sale, involving real money and prices contributed some dynamic practice experience for many children who were cashiers, took in money, made change and afterward, helped total the money, making piles of ten, finding money equivalences, and adding and comparing totals. Toward the end of the study, the question of change was raised again and Harold said, "When you give the checker too much money, he has to give you some back." While this clear conception of change was not shared by all the children, there was evidence of growing understanding of the concept by many. The problem of pricing was more difficult. Somehow, empty cans and food containers rarely arrived in school with a discernible price stamp. Sometimes, the teacher suggested suitable prices for commodities and the children pasted gummed labels on cans and wrote these prices.

> One day, the School Secretary entered the room before nine o'clock and, seeing four children at store play, remarked that she thought she would do her marketing. She ordered four items for which Henry

charged her six dollars. She protested that it was too expensive, that she thought she ought to get at least six items for six dollars, not just four. Henry suggested she pay three dollars instead.

On another day, Eddie handed David two quarts of milk when the latter had only ordered one. As David rejected the second milk carton, Eddie waved the paper bill he had just received from David, shouting, "Well, one quart doesn't cost a hundred dollars."

Phoebe was a canny customer, and, when David charged her ten dollars for a can of soup, she said, "Then I won't buy any." "Well, then two dollars," David compromised.

The group discussed, "How do you figure prices?" with the supermarket manager when he visited the class. Cookie prices for the children's sale had been determined by vote.

The supermarket manager told the children they never voted on prices in the store though they often discussed them. He stressed the need for food prices to be sufficiently attractive so that customers would buy and not go elsewhere. He also stressed the need for the store to make money. Competitive prices were discussed, as well as price changes. He told the children a store could not stay in business if there was no money left over, and therefore prices had to be higher than the cost to the store.

Complex elements of the pricing structure could not be grasped by the children on first acquaintance. But the basic and important concept of a pricing process did emerge, with the understanding that somehow "prices are figured." This first, global stage of conceptualization is the most difficult of all stages. This involves the initial perception and cognition of some meanings of a concept, which constitutes the necessary base for further learnings, new experiences, and more complex organization of the relationships and understandings involved.

THE CONCEPT
OF PROFIT

The concept of profit proved to be confusing to these five-year-olds. It had been thought that the concept would begin to have meaning for the children if they *failed* to make a profit in a cookie sale. A negative result was expected to stimulate the children to raise questions to try to understand their failure to achieve a profit, while a positive result might simply have been taken for granted. Hence, the children were permitted to vote on a price per cookie, set at two cents, which did not cover costs.

Costs were simplified to the tangible costs of ingredients purchased at the store. Four groups of children made purchases at the supermarket, then reported to each other on the items, quantities, and prices, reading cash register tapes while unloading their grocery bags. The teacher totaled the four subtotals and emphasized the sum in various ways, such as by writing it on the chalkboard and referring to it and mentioning it on several occasions. But when the money receipts of the cookie sale were totaled, the children remembered neither that money had been spent on the ingredients nor how much. They could not understand that, despite the sizable money intake, the cookie sale had resulted in a net loss instead of a profit. When asked if they had made a profit, they pointed to the money intake. They found it difficult to relate this intake to the larger sums previously spent at the store for ingredients. Had the teacher omitted these searching questions and discussions, it might have been erroneously assumed that the children had learned this complicated concept, when in fact they had not.

When the extent of the children's confusions about profit was revealed, it seemed necessary to plan a clearer opportunity to discover some meanings of the concept. It was decided to hold another sale which would yield a profit instead of a loss. This profit was to be embodied in tangible form by being turned into a treat for the class. Costs were to be held to a single dollar, which was to be borrowed from and subsequently returned to someone who often visited the class. Since the sale was to be held the week before the spring recess, it was decided to sell hard-boiled eggs for the children to decorate.

The egg sale was orderly and efficient. Children manned the store and sold each other eggs, carefully counting out pennies. Most children brought the exact amount, six cents, but some children required change from dimes and this was negotiated by the few children who could make the computations. The children took turns, in small groups, helping to total the money intake. During several discussions which followed, the children seemed to understand that the forty cents left over after the return of the borrowed dollar constituted profit. The class voted to buy jelly beans with their profit.

This time the concept of profit seemed fairly well understood. Even those children who did not comprehend the figures seemed to perceive the gross result—that there was money left over. The class enjoyed their jelly-bean profit, recalling the egg sale and the money quantities involved. But confusion about profit reappeared about two weeks later.

The teacher read a story to the class about a child who went to the store to buy eggs so that her mother could bake her a birthday cake. In the ensuing discussion, the children confused the change which the storekeeper gave her with profit. As the teacher asked more questions, more confusion was apparent.

> Another discussion touched on profit when the children were given copies of a cookie recipe to take home, and the teacher asked the children, "Was our cookie sale a success?"
>
> "It was too noisy," said Margaret.
>
> "A success means people came to buy our cookies," Jimmy explained.
>
> "Even if I wasn't there, I'm sure it was success," Pat said enthusiastically. "I like sugar cookies."
>
> "People came," said the teacher. "Did a lot of money come in?"
>
> "Lots of money," contributed one child.
>
> But when the teacher asked whether there had been a profit on the cookie sale, the children were not sure.

The visit of the supermarket manager contributed some information to the study of profit when he told the children that if his store bought and sold a product for the same price, it could not stay in business, that groceries had to be sold for more than they cost to buy from farmers and other wholesale dealers. But he did not otherwise define profit, nor did he refer to its residual character. Soon afterwards, David said that he had been playing store, at evaluation time.

> "Were you the manager?" said the teacher.
>
> "Yes," said David.
>
> "You took in a lot of money today. Could you keep all that?"
>
> "He keeps money to buy food from the farmers," said Marty.
>
> "He keeps money to buy food for his children," said Jimmy indicating some further confusion of profit with salary.
>
> "He puts money in the bank," said Sheila.

"He pays the rest of the people in the store," said Laura.
"Does he have any money left over?"
"Yes," chorused the group.
"What is this leftover money called?"
"That is his profit," said Jimmy.
"He has to keep some money in the cash drawer for the people who give money," said Marty, indicating a good grasp of the change-making concept.

While this discussion was far from a clear delineation of the concept of profit, it indicated a growing knowledge of the notion of costs and of the residual nature of profit. There was still confusion and indication of the need for many more experiences and opportunities over long periods of time to verbalize and clarify these emerging understandings.

DIVISION OF LABOR

The concept of division of labor is in some respects a very complicated one with its concomitants of lower unit costs, increased mass production, automation, and huge capital outlays in plant and equipment. It was thought that only a very small part of this "big idea" could be conveyed to five-year-olds in their first round with this concept. However, a vivid experience which could convey some meaning would provide a good base for further learnings and "revisiting" the idea at higher grade levels.

One experience was planned to dramatize this concept, and the basic idea it sought to convey was that more things could be produced if a job could be broken into small tasks. A group of people could produce more together, each performing one small task, than if each person tried to produce the whole product himself. It was the week before Spring vacation, and the children were making holiday decorations and coloring eggs. Up to this point, no decision had been made as to what task to use for this purpose. After discussing various possibilities, the researcher and the teacher agreed that it would be seasonal and appropriate to make paper flower-baskets and that the general idea of division of labor could be grasped from such an activity.

First the assembled class was shown the technique of making a very simple, handled, paper basket. The children each made one, and these were admired and put aside to be filled with candy later. Then the class was told that there would be a race to see whether children who continued to work alone could produce more baskets than children who worked together as a team. Asked to hypothesize which would produce more baskets, the children overwhelmingly voted in favor of those working alone. Since it had taken about fifteen minutes to make individual baskets, it was decided to limit the race to a fifteen-minute period. This time, the group was divided into three teams of six children each, with another child appointed by the teacher to be the group "supervisor," to keep the team supplied with paper, paste, and scissors. Two groups were to work individually as before, while one group was to divide the total task among the members of the team so that one child was to cut handle strips, another to cut slits to make corners while another pasted some decorative flowers. Ellen, who was supervisor for the table where division of labor was being demonstrated, became aware of the bottlenecks at her table. She noticed that handles took longer to paste than corners and so she helped to redistribute the tasks at her table for more efficient cooperation.

The children enjoyed the race, and all worked earnestly. Several children remarked that you were supposed to work just as carefully during the race as you had the first time. The children agreed that sloppy work would not be acceptable.

When time was called, the children were assembled and the three supervisors were asked to report on results. Steve reported that his group of six children, working individually, had made six baskets. Barbara's report was the same. Ellen reported that her group had worked as a team, dividing up the tasks, and that, in this group of six children, twelve baskets had been produced.

It was pointed out that the paper-basket-making race did not turn out as expected. The hypothesis, tested in direct experimentation, was disproved. The class was asked to state what the experiment showed.

"The children who worked together and helped each other made the most baskets," Jimmy summarized.

Several children alluded to this experience in other contexts in the following weeks, always remembering the results correctly. Unlike the experience with the concept of profit, the discrepancy between the hypothesis and the results was readily remembered. Perhaps in this case the concept was more clearly presented and since it was unlike any of the other concepts studied it was not confused with other concepts but could be remembered clearly.

THE CONCEPT
OF FAMILIES

The concept of a family seems very close to the young child's experience, but it is not necessarily obvious in its meaning. Since the study assumed the family as the basic consuming unit, it was planned to focus on the meaning of a family and on family size, composition, and variation. In addition, this topic was chosen as an appropriate one with which to explore the children's ability to understand and interpret the symbolism of a graph.

The problem was to make the child conscious of his own family size and composition, of its similarity to and difference from other families, and of the distribution of different kinds of families within the class population. Some simple ways of representing and symbolizing this distribution were also planned. The concept of families was introduced in the first week of the study with the expectation of reviewing and expanding the initial ideas several times during the study. Actually, so many projects were under way in the class that it was difficult to follow through on all plans and this one was not picked up again until the last week of the study, except for occasional allusions to families in discussions.

In the first discussion of the concept, children were asked to tell in turn, "Who lives with you in your house?" In effect, this was the definition of the family which was to be used. The need for recording the information in some form, to preserve it for further use, was dramatized when the class tried to remember how many children lived with families of a mother, a father, and four children or with families of different sizes and composition. The second time, the children repeated their family descriptions and tallies on the chalkboard were made for each family type, as follows:

Family Type[9]	Number Represented in Class
| |	X
| | |	X X X X
| | | |	X X X X X X
| | | | |	X X X X X X X X
| | | | | |	X X X
| | | |	X X X

This was followed by a discussion which sought to generalize the information as to what constitutes a family.

Dorothy said, "There can't be just one in a family."

Eddie said, "Two is a family."

In reply to the question whether families had to be any special size, several children insisted that families had to be the same as their own. These children were referred to the chalkboard tally, which was explained several times. This could be termed "reality testing," since the children were referred to evidence which contradicted their incorrect assertions.

It was also agreed that a family could not consist only of children because there had to be at least one adult to care for them.

The next day, instead of representing families by short and long chalk strokes, construction paper figures were taped to the board, a large, blue, male figure for the father or any adult male, large, pink, female figures for adult females, and small, yellow, child-like figures to represent children. Six groups of paper figures now represented the six family types in the class, at intervals across the chalkboard. The children were asked to line up in front of their own family types, with some help from the teacher. Each row was counted and it was noted how the families were distributed in the class.

Again it was hoped to make the children conscious of the need to record and preserve information. While the children were still on lines, they were asked whether they could stay there for a week or

[9] The taller strokes represent adults; the shorter strokes represent children in the column headed *Family Type*. Each X in the next column represents a child in the class belonging to a family of the type represented on the left.

two, so that the information could be available for discussion another time. There was much laughter and such protests as, "We'd get hungry and tired," and "We'd get sleepy." Since the children could not suggest any way to remember how many children were on each line, that is, how many children had each family type, they were asked, "Could we use something *instead of you* so you won't have to stand in line for a long time?" The purpose of this discussion was to highlight the need for symbols of some kind.

The children suggested many objects which could be used to replace themselves, including string, dolls, chairs, bowls, cats (although it was objected that cats would run away), dogs (with the proviso that they be tied down so that they could not run away), paper clips, toy trucks, and other toys. Pianos were suggested but were rejected by several children as too big and expensive. It was agreed that most of the suggestions were practical, but, since blocks were available in quantity, these could be used by each child, instead of himself.

Each child took a block from the shelves, in turn, and piled it on the floor just below the paper family figures which were still taped to the chalkboard. It was stressed that the child was placing the block to take his place on the line. The piles were counted several times by different children and the sums were checked against the chalkboard tally. However, the blocks had to be put away because the kindergarten room was used for other purposes in the afternoon. The problem was posed as to what could be used instead of blocks which would not have to be put away.

It was assumed that some children had not understood all of the discussion about using blocks "instead of you," so it was decided to repeat this activity, to permit more children to become aware of the meaning of the substitution of the blocks. This time, the tallies were somewhat different because the children were sharpening their understanding of the definition of a family being used.

One child explained her grandmother did not live in her house, and therefore her family belonged to the two-adult, two-child category, instead of the three-adult, two-child category. Again, the problem was presented of finding a substitute for blocks which would not have to be put away. Suggestions were made to write on the chalkboard or on paper, and it was agreed that the information would eventually be written on paper. However, a flannel board was introduced as another way to indicate information about families, which would not have to be put away.

The flannel board was used in order to introduce another step on the way to abstraction and symbolism. A flannel horizontal bar was placed across the bottom of the flannel board to represent the floor on which the blocks had been piled the day before. Flannel figures were used to represent the construction paper figures, a large flannel figure representing either an adult male or female, a small flannel figure representing a child and a flannel block representing the real blocks. Groups of flannel figures comprising each family type were placed below the floor line for their own family types. It was stressed that the flannel blocks were in place of the real blocks which were "instead of you."

When the children were asked to look carefully at the completed flannel board, to see what it tells us, they looked puzzled. One child touched the flannel board and said, "It's soft and it's flannel."

But when the question was rephrased, "What can we find out from the flannel board," Pat said, "It shows the different kinds of families." Several children identified different kinds of families represented on the flannel board, counting the number of flannel blocks to ascertain the number of such families in the class.

To clarify the meaning of the family, several cases were tested against the definition. When asked whether one, single, adult-sized figure constituted a family, Steve said it was not a family because it had no children. In the class, every family had at least one child.

The researcher asked, "When you grow up and get married, will your father and mother be a family by themselves?"

"No," said Pat, "because they'll be dead."

"They could be grandfathers and grandmothers for your children," Jimmy said. Most of the children then agreed that two adults could be a family.

During the last week of the study, when it had been decided to review the work on the concept of families and to work further toward symbolization, the researcher started to tape the construction paper figures to the blackboard. Several children, recognizing them, said playfully, "Not that again!" The children recalled the procedure during the first phase of the project and asked, "Will we have to line up again?" and "Will we use blocks again?"

There was repetition of the work with blocks, chalkboard tallies, and the flannel board. The children remembered very clearly that blocks were "instead of you," pointing to themselves. This time, Margaret, noting that one family type had only a mother and a child, stated that there had to be a father for a child to be born. The researcher pointed out that sometimes the father goes away or there is a divorce. One child added, "Or the father dies." Sheila said, "Sometimes they don't even get married." It was agreed that a mother and a child could be a family, since it was more than one and had an adult, which met the requirements of our definition. There seemed to be even greater interest in the repetition of the work, than in the initial project, and some children refused to go home when they were called for, until they could show their mothers the flannel board and explain its meaning.

Two days later, it was decided to introduce the bar graph as another way of representing the data about the families in the class. It was planned to have a discussion on this during the last half hour of the morning. The researcher sat at a table at about ten o'clock in the morning, constructing the bar graph with crayons while the children were engaged in cleaning up before going out to play. Several children, as they finished tidying up, clustered about the researcher and watched her, while waiting for the rest of the class. Dorothy, Sheila, Margaret, Steve, and several other children kept asking the researcher what she was doing and she said she would tell them about it later. Dorothy and Margaret started guessing. They guessed that the long and short lines represented adults and children and they guessed that the bars in the graph represented the blocks, the flannel blocks, and the children and the numbers indicated how many children had each family type. Other children began to identify their family types and the distinctive types which were represented by only one child each, naming the child who belonged in the category. The class then went outdoors.

Late in the morning, there was a brief discussion with the whole class. Pat promptly identified correctly all the elements of the graph. Children were asked to stand when their family type was pointed to on the graph and most children complied correctly. The researcher counted the number in the vertical column at the left and asked why there were numbers only to seven. "We didn't need any more," Pat said. "If there had been nine children who had such a family, we could have numbers eight and nine."

The student teacher had missed this discussion and, when she returned, she said she did not understand the graph and would like to have it explained. One at a time, each of several children gave her a brief but understandable explanation, using very similar terms as she afterwards reported. There were thus a variety of indications that a considerable amount of understanding had occurred about family size, composition and variation and some simple ways to symbolize quantitative information.

The study ended with the use of a hand-operated ice-cream freezer in class to make ice cream and to stimulate a final discussion about producers. The children enjoyed producing the ice cream almost as much as they enjoyed consuming it; meanwhile they chatted freely and somewhat knowledgeably about producers.

BIBLIOGRAPHY

First Stories to Read Aloud, New York: Wonder Books, 1959.

Furman, Dorothy W., "Content, Trends and Topics in the Social Studies," *Social Studies in Elementary Schools*, Thirty-Second Yearbook of the National Council for the Social Studies, National Education Association, Washington, D.C., 1962.

Jersild, Arthur T., and Ruth J. Tasch, *Children's Interests and What They Suggest for Education*, New York: Teachers College Press, Teachers College, Columbia University, 1949.

Mitchell, Lucy Sprague, *Our Children and Our Schools*, New York: Simon and Schuster, 1950.

National Task Force on Economic Education, *Economic Education in the Schools*, New York: Committee for Economic Development, 1961.

Puner, Helen Walker, *Daddies, What They Do All Day*, New York: Lothrop, Lee and Shepard, 1946.

Robison, Helen F., "Learning Economic Concepts in the Kindergarten," unpublished Ed.D. Project, Teachers College, Columbia University, 1963.

Strauss, Anselm L., "The Development and Transformation of Monetary Meanings in the Child," *American Sociological Review*, 1952, 17:275–286.

4

CONTENT FROM THE SOCIAL SCIENCE DISCIPLINES

Teachers and other curriculum workers who desire to define the content of the kindergarten curriculum in terms of basic concepts from significant bodies of knowledge will find an increasing measure of help coming from scholars in the separate disciplines. This has not always been so. For many years, the emphasis in the content fields has been on outlines of facts and information to be learned. An obviously impractical approach in view of today's explosion of knowledge, the emphasis on factual detail never has resulted in truly basic learning. This approach has stopped short of helping learners to see what the facts and information add up to in terms of basic concepts which provide a framework for understanding and for dealing with the social and physical world.

The growing interest in looking to the structures of the disciplines for guidance in choosing curriculum experiences for learners at many levels in recent years has resulted in a number of efforts to define more clearly the structure of certain bodies of knowledge. Much remains to be done by scholars before the social sciences will have been fully defined in terms of basic concepts. But kindergarten educators can find significant help in this direction in their selection of content at this time. This chapter and the following one are devoted to a discussion of the status of work in a number of the bodies of knowledge from which kindergarten program content can be drawn.

BASIC CONCEPTS FROM
THE SOCIAL SCIENCES

A number of attempts are being made to define the social science disciplines, including history, geography, economics, sociology, political science, and anthropology. A broad look at the social science fields for high school study is found in *The Social Studies and the Social Sciences*.[1] Initial attempts to develop basic concepts are also available in some separate fields. The report of the National Task Force on Economic Education[2] was the first of these. In the field of geography, a recent publication of the National Council for Geographic Education not only lists the basic elements in geography, but also translates these ideas into suggested curricula for each level of education.[3] A recent doctoral study in history education provides a similar base for determining the key elements in this field.[4] The spadework now being done in the social sciences promises that soon-to-be needed conceptual frameworks will be available.

There is really no danger that academic scholars working independently to conceptualize their fields will be at cross purposes with each other. Variety in end-products can be fruitful and provocative for scholars and teachers. Common elements in different conceptual structures begin to be identified and to suggest paths to more useful results. As these conceptual bases are tested in school, teachers will be able to determine their usefulness. None of the statements should be considered the last word. By their very nature, the social science fields are open to a variety of definitions and are constantly being redefined. This should not deter teachers who are concerned with developing programs for concept development. One must make use

[1] American Council of Learned Societies and the National Council for the Social Studies, *The Social Studies and the Social Sciences*, New York: Harcourt, Brace and World, 1962.

[2] Report of the National Task Force on Economic Education, *Economic Education in the Schools*, New York: Committee for Economic Development, 1961.

[3] Wilhelmina Hill (Ed.), *Curriculum Guide for Geographic Education*, Norman, Okla.: National Council for Geographic Education, 1963.

[4] David Loucks Elliott, "Curriculum Development and History as a Discipline," unpublished Ed.D. Project, Teachers College, Columbia University, 1963.

of whatever is available, knowing that improvements will continue to be made. The process itself, however, is of such value that even a program developed from a tentative set of basic concepts permits teachers to offer children significant learning.

History

One useful attempt to organize the basic concepts in history indicates the elements of historical method and defines the ways in which the historians study the past. The above-mentioned study by Elliott points out that the term "history" is defined in at least four ways: "(1) the unrecoverable totality of the past—the past as actuality; (2) the records and remains of that totality; (3) written or spoken history, the image we form of the past; and (4) the process by which history comes to be." [5] Since operating with four definitions is confusing, Elliott has selected "the image we form of the past" as best representing what historians attempt to create and what students are asked to build for themselves.

The historian deals with a data source that can never be replicated. It is impossible to recreate the past. It is only possible to study evidence of past events, in such forms as original documents and records, artifacts, realia, archeological remains, and spoken or written descriptions by witnesses. In forming an image of the past, the historian uses concepts, theories, and inquiry tools from other bodies of knowledge, such as economics, geography, and archeology. History, as Elliott sees it, is a distinctive kind of knowledge in that trends seen separately from the perspectives of other disciplines can be synthesized in historical perspective. The historian seeks relationships, attributing causality and continuity to events, but, as a historian, he cannot abstract laws, since it is beyond the scope of his discipline to do so. For example, he may be able to specify the causes of a specific political revolution but he does not generalize from this to develop a law governing all political revolutions.

In interpreting the remains of the past, the historian is constantly locating, evaluating, and criticizing data sources, attempting to determine the validity and reliability of these sources. Thus a prime problem for the historian is to determine how much confidence to

[5] *Ibid.*, p. 96.

place in any piece of evidence about the past. But this is only a beginning. The historian also places events in a framework of time, utilizing chronology—with its related concepts of change, continuity, and progress—in his attempt to understand the past.

In dealing with the relationships among historical data, the historian is constantly interpreting the facts of history. He does this by approaching the data sources of history with hypotheses, testing these hypotheses against the available evidence. Interpretation may involve explanation, attempts to assign causes to events, and/or grouping events into meaningful periods in which certain trends may be noted or new ones may be forecast.

Although interpretation is an important element in history, there is no single "right" way to interpret any set of past events. History is written from many different perspectives and contains a variety of interpretations and meanings. Multiple interpretations complement each other and enrich our understanding of the past. History is also revised frequently as new evidence and new points of view develop.

The four key concepts of history Elliott has isolated are:

1. *Chronology*—the ordering of events in sequence, usually within a framework of calendar dates.
2. *Periodization*—the clustering of single events into larger events or periods.
3. *Interpretation*—the ordering and interrelation of past events and conditions.
4. *Multanimity*—the coexistence of multiple interpretative approaches drawn from other major disciplines.[6]

It can be seen that, because of the nature of history as a body of knowledge and its interpretation and use of knowledge and concepts from other bodies of knowledge, these four key concepts differ somewhat from key concepts in other disciplines. Elliott's concepts appear to define the nature of historical inquiry or the ways in which historians confirm or discover new knowledge, that is, the process by which historians develop history. This process can be defined so that students can be guided in forming their own images of man's past.

Chronology and time concepts are rather abstract for young

[6] *Ibid.*, pp. 92–153.

children, but interpretation and periodization may be introduced in many different ways. The geography–history study described in Chapter 2 suggested some ways to begin to introduce historical concepts through the use of physical time-lines; a visit to a museum to study artifacts, costumes, and dioramas representing New York City in the past; comparisons of contemporary and "old-fashioned" ships; and pictures and maps of the city.

Other suggestions, made elsewhere in this book, include the use of creative dramatics, with costumes and props, to project characters and events of the past, especially on themes of well-known historical characters in American history, such as Christopher Columbus, George Washington, and Abraham Lincoln; visiting older houses or buildings in the community which retain some visible characteristics of prior times, consulting local historical associations for location of such buildings or of artifacts, or of older citizens who have personal information of historical interest of a bygone era, as well as such sources as pictures, photographs, books, filmstrips, and movies.

The historian's mode of inquiry, the "historical method," can be practiced in primitive form by a class in pursuit of information about the recent past. The teacher can stress problems of interpretation, validity of information sources and contradictory information.

Family albums can sometimes serve to bring the recent past to life, as children identify relatives strangely garbed in old-fashioned clothing, sometimes pictured in rural settings which can now be identified as suburban or urban. Children beg their parents for stories of their childhood days and are almost as intensely interested in stories about the childhood experiences of teachers; such stories often have much historical interest.

When local data sources about the recent past seem scarce, a surprising amount can often be turned up by letting the community know about the search, through such devices as letters to parents, a classroom or school newspaper, letters to the editor of the local newspaper or to town or city officials. Involving children in this process provides a powerful learning experience which cannot be duplicated in other ways. The teacher might consult U.S. Bureau of Census figures on population for the community, in order to pinpoint times of rapid change within the community, either of population increase or decline.

Studying the recent historical past of a community provides an excellent framework within which to incorporate some of the geographic concepts and skills suggested in the next section. Geography and history concepts can often be developed together for the young child in a concrete neighborhood framework which is familiar to him.

Geography

In geography there have been two fruitful attempts to identify basic concepts, which have much in common. James states that, ". . . geography examines the relationships not only between man and his habitat, but also between man and the various cultural features resulting from economic, social, or political processes." [7] Thus, physical and cultural aspects of geography which James has listed include, for example, the concept of *areal association* or the selection of ". . . those physical, biotic, and cultural features that are tied together causally, and which give distinctive character to an area on the earth's surface . . . ." [8] Other concepts James has defined include the *regional concept*,[9] *the teaching of maps*,[10] and *the use of the culture concept in geography*.[11]

Warman's listing of basic concepts in geography is somewhat different but closely related to James'. The nine concepts that Warman identifies are "globalism," "the round earth on flat paper," "the life layer," "areal distinctions—differences and likenesses," "the region," "resources culturally defined," "man the chooser," "spatial interaction," and "perpetual transformation." [12]

While it is to be expected that social scientists will not have reached

[7] Preston E. James, "Geography," in American Council of Learned Societies and the National Council for the Social Studies, *op. cit.*, p. 48.

[8] *Ibid.*, p. 49.

[9] *Ibid.*, p. 51.

[10] *Ibid.*, p. 58.

[11] *Ibid.*, p. 70.

[12] Henry J. Warman, "Major Concepts in Geography," in Wilhelmina Hill, *op. cit.*, p. 25.

consensus about the basic concepts in their field, it is interesting to note the extent of similarity and overlapping in these two conceptual-izations of geography. Both view physical and cultural geography as inseparable aspects of man's occupation of physical space and both regard man as the key to geographic understanding. Regional analysis in terms of contrasts and common features is basic to both conceptual schemes. Being geographers, both underline the importance and relevance of the special tools of the geographer, map and globe skills, to geographic learning.

Barton is a geographer who has developed a helpful listing of geographic skills children can learn in "an activities-centered class-room and with the out-of-doors geography laboratory" which may suggest some experiences for children which help to develop basic concepts, as follows:

1. developing a sense of space and time-distance;
2. observing, identifying, recording and interpreting out-of-doors data, scenes and landscapes;
3. identifying geographic specimens and scenes within buildings;
4. making, reading and interpreting maps and reading and interpreting globes;
5. taking, reading and interpreting pictures; and
6. making, reading and interpreting models and graphic forms such as sketches, diagrams, graphs, profiles, cross-sections and three-dimen-sional illustrations.[13]

This is a very suggestive list of "doing" activities, listing behaviors which children can begin to practice. For the five-year-old, it includes many appropriate manipulative and observational activities, of which numerous examples are given later in this chapter.

Economics

In the field of economics there have been several attempts to distill the basic concepts. A recent authoritative effort was the report of the National Task Force on Economic Education.[14] While this report represents the first consensus by a group of scholars in the social science field, its lack of provision for testing the program

---

[13] Thomas Frank Barton, "Geography Skills and Techniques," in Wilhelmina Hill, *op. cit.*, p. 54.

[14] National Task Force on Economic Education, *op. cit.*

in schools may be a serious weakness. Unless bridges are built between academic scholars and schools, in a dynamic process of interchange, much valuable material may be lost to teachers.

Senesh, however, is an economist who has worked jointly with a school system to develop and test a program of economic education, which is eventually to cover grades from one to twelve. He has listed five generalizations as the basis for what he calls an "organic curriculum" in economics, as follows:

1. All people and all nations are confronted with the conflict between their unlimited wants and limited resources. The degree of the conflict may vary but the conflict is always present.

2. From the beginning, men have tried new ways and means to lessen the gap between unlimited wants and limited resources. Their efforts to invent new machines and improve production processes are evidence of the desire to produce more, better, and faster.

3. In all countries the basic questions to be answered are: what goods and services will be produced; how much of these will be produced; how will they be produced—that is, with more men or more machines or more raw materials and who will receive the goods and services?

4. In the United States what and how much will be produced, how much of these will be produced, and for whom are largely determined by the free choices of the American people, either as consumers or as participants in the production process.

5. Through their political process, the American people sometimes limit their individual free choices in order to increase the general welfare.[15]

Using these five generalizations as a point of departure, Senesh has worked with teachers and curriculum experts to develop statements of understandings to be taught by grade levels. The program is especially promising because of this collaboration with the school system, the practical procedures developed, the evaluative techniques in use, and the expectation that feedback from the schools will continuously improve the program. Instructional materials developed through this program are becoming available for general distribution. It will be noted that the study on developing some economic concepts with kindergarten children, reported in Chapter 3, avoided formal teaching procedures and workbooks as inappropriate for five-year-olds, generally.

It should also be noted that the National Task Force Report on

[15] Lawrence Senesh, "The Organic Curriculum: A New Experiment in Economic Education," *The Councilor*, 1960, 21(1):45.

Economic Education starts with a listing of generalizations similar to Senesh's but develops key concepts in some detail, for use primarily at the high school level. Teachers can use the Task Force Report both for their own understanding, and in order to develop from it some concepts to be used with younger children, as described in Chapter 1.

Sociology

One sociologist defines sociology as the study of society ". . . viewed as a system, as a set of interacting parts." [16] Sykes calls the central concern of sociology its "functional orientation," or ". . . how the activities of men function to maintain or change the social system in which they live." [17] While Sykes does not identify the key concepts or the basic structure of sociology, he describes some of the most important functions all societies serve, which tend to be requisite for the continuation of the group. For example, one such basic function is socialization; Sykes points out ". . . and so in every society there is the problem of teaching children the values, skills, knowledge, and other requirements, for the survival of society." [18]

Another definition of sociology, which may help teachers to differentiate its content from other social sciences, states that sociology is ". . . the discipline that describes the phenomena that are created by the social interaction of human beings and the manner in which these phenomena affect the behavior of individuals." [19]

Another sociologist has defined the terms sociologists use in their analyses and since all sociologists deal with these terms, teachers may find them useful in planning for experiences with children to develop some significant understandings. For example, Rose defines a social group as ". . . a number of biological individuals who have a system of common expectations in their minds." [20] These expec-

[16] Gresham M. Sykes, "Sociology," in American Council of Learned Societies et al., *op cit.*, p. 160.

[17] *Ibid.*, p. 160.

[18] *Ibid.*, p. 163.

[19] Don Martindale and Elio D. Monachesi, *Elements of Sociology*, New York: Harper and Brothers, 1951, p. 39.

[20] Arnold M. Rose, *Sociology, the Study of Human Relations*, New York: Alfred A. Knopf, 1957, p. 32.

tations arise out of a history of common experience and make it possible for a group of individuals to understand each other, to know how to behave toward each other and to know what people expect of each other. The integrated group, according to Rose, has the basic characteristic ". . . that each member is able imaginatively to take the role of the other, in advance of action, and so adjust his behavior to that of the other." [21] Rose contrasts the integrated group with the crowd, which ". . . may be defined as a group of individuals in physical proximity to each other and influencing each other through the mere fact of their physical proximity." [22]

Another important concept in sociology is the concept of "self." According to Rose, "This idea of self has three elements: (1) the imagination of our appearance to the other person; (2) the imagination of his judgment of the appearance; (3) our reaction to that imagined judgment, such as a feeling of pride or of mortification." [23] Thus, each person as he matures develops a concept of "me," which may be largely but not entirely his conception of how others view him.

Rose's definition of culture is parallel to the social group, that is, "The important idea in the concept of culture is that there are common understandings as to how individuals are to behave toward each other." [24] The social group, therefore, consists of the specific individuals who share common understandings about behavior, or who share the culture. He has defined social process as ". . . a characteristic series of social changes occurring to a person or group in which one step develops out of the previous one." [25] Sociologists have catalogued hundreds of different social processes, which change as societies change. Examples of social processes which are studied by sociologists are socialization, conflict, individualization, diffusion, migration and revolution.

Rose's definitions clearly suggest the structure which he would be likely to identify, should he go on to define the key concepts in sociology. Cataloguing the key concepts in sociology should help to

[21] *Ibid.*, p. 267.
[22] *Ibid.*, p. 268.
[23] *Ibid.*, pp. 48–49.
[24] *Ibid.*, p. 33.
[25] *Ibid.*, p. 565.

indicate the extent of overlap with other social sciences. For example, both sociology and economics are concerned with the production and distribution of goods and services, although economic analysis differs somewhat from sociological analysis in theory and methodology.

Some of the basic sociological terms defined above are concepts with which kindergarten children can deal directly in some respects. For example, the concept of self may be explored by focusing on the question, "Who Am I?" By this process, the young child can actually make conscious efforts to differentiate himself from others since, essentially, one knows oneself only in relationship to others. Such explorations might include drawing self-portraits, dictating autobiographies to be written by the teacher, and discussing children's behavior in different situations. Such discussions might raise questions such as "Are you the same at home as you are in school?" or "Do you behave differently playing in the street than playing in school?"

Other ways of helping a child to pursue a conscious sense of self may include enumeration of family members and relationships to the child, making slides of children's photographs to view and discuss in class, contrasting children in the class on the bases of height, weight, and hair and eye color, and comparing children in the class as to preferences in foods, television programs, and games. In this way, children may learn that families vary as to size and composition, and their own may be different from many others in the class; that, while all children have the same nutritional needs, there is considerable diversity in adequate menus; and that, while children in a class may wear similar clothes, each child has a unique set of physical characteristics which make him recognizable in a photograph as well as in person. Many different experiences can help a child to develop a strong sense of self.

Taking photographs of children in classroom activities or on trips and discussing these photographs or slides in the context of the activity is another way in which teachers help children to see themselves in other contexts. This helps the child to differentiate himself from others as well as to see himself as the same individual in different settings. Some teachers use a large mirror in the housekeeping corner in which children view themselves either in everyday clothes or occasionally in dress-up clothes or costumes. On Hallowe'en, children like to hide behind their masks and play, "Guess who I am."

The concept of the *integrated group* can also be explored by young children. As the children enter school in September they represent more of a mass than a group. The process by which this mass of children becomes an integrated group can be shown by contrasting their group behavior at the beginning of the year with behavior in similar situations later in the term. This is also a way in which the teacher helps children to notice their social progress and to take pride in their social achievements. The children could become aware of and begin to analyze the various groups in which they hold membership, such as families and friendships, to learn that they belong to a variety of groups and that they do not share all of their group memberships with all their classmates. They can also begin to see the similarities and differences between groups.

Social processes evolve in the kindergarten, as well as in all other aspects of life with which the young child is familiar. Kindergarten education itself is part of the socialization process. In the microcosmic society of the classroom, such processes as conflict, accommodation, and communication occur. To the degree that the teacher can help children become aware of these processes, they can be studied. The processes observed in the classroom can be compared with similar processes occurring in other social situations.

Culture is a concept that kindergarten children can begin to grasp. Children are aware of the special ways some things are done in their families and the special meanings that certain symbols hold for them. Often major holidays can be a way of making cultural similarities and differences noticed. In a healthy context in which each child is respected and valued, these events can be used to provide examples of cultural diversity. Other situations in the children's daily lives could furnish similar resources upon which understandings can be built.

It can be concluded that teachers can find many fruitful ways to guide children toward some basic sociological understandings. Program designs, however, will surely improve as sociologists furnish clearer statements of these key ideas.

Political Science

Political science is another social science in which key concepts have yet to be formulated. Long has looked at political science education in terms of its objectives or goals rather than its basic ideas.[26] Traditionally, the elementary schools have chiefly been interested in political science content for its contributions to education for good citizenship. Some interest has been developing in comparison and evaluation of different political systems and processes at upper grade levels where it is becoming fashionable to study "the world" in addition to our own country.

The formulation of goals in political science education may provide the impetus needed to study and identify the basic understandings in political science. Classroom and school situations may be excellent bases for children's initial experiences with political science concepts and may foster greater consciousness and interest in political processes, with experience and maturation. The development of content from political science for children's study should also add pressure to the demand for more unified approaches to social science concepts.

Anthropology

One anthropologist sees anthropology as playing a twofold role in the social studies. The first role is to serve as a supplier of prehistoric and cross-cultural data for the other social sciences.[27] This includes information about man before history was written and comparisons of different kinds of societies, such as stone age and industrialized societies. This kind of information and understandings chiefly serves as a resource for other social sciences, clarifying and illuminating them.

Oliver sees anthropology in another role as a distinct body of knowledge and theory.[28] This discipline, or body of knowledge, is concerned with: "The structure and function of the behavior systems

[26] Norton E. Long, "Political Science," in American Council of Learned Societies et al., *op. cit.*, pp. 88–105.

[27] *Ibid.*, p. 136.

[28] *Ibid.*

comprising human societies," and "The connections between bio-logical make-up of human beings and their habitual behavior systems," according to Oliver.[29] His formulation and development of some basic understandings in this field should provide a solid basis upon which anthropologists can build to develop formulations more detailed and therefore more useful to teachers. Anthropological-sociological ideas might be initiated in the kindergarten around such topics as cultural pluralism, appreciation of ethnic differences, differences in national cuisines, costumes, housing patterns, and languages. The more ethnic variety represented by children in the class, the easier is the teacher's task in helping children to note and experience a variety of human institutions, national holidays, and vocational and recreational differences.

For example, this television-reared generation of young children is often aware of such variations in human institutions and behavior as eskimos' rubbing noses instead of kissing, of Asian people who shake their own hands instead of touching other people, as well as climatic effects upon peoples' dress and housing. These studies can be brought closer to home, and made more personal, when families in the school or community represent much diversity in food preferences or in recreational or other behavior patterns. Needless to say, studies of this kind must be devoid of moralistic or judg-mental factors and must truly seek to appreciate variety and difference.

In many classrooms, no such variety is represented, but since we are a nation of immigrants, there may be family treasures or heir-looms in the community, such as hand-embroidered clothing, brass samovars, hand-made shepherd's flutes, and other distinctive arti-facts of ways of life somewhat different from contemporary American urban society. When these cannot be elicited from the community, the resources of museums, books, and encyclopedias may be explored with a view to finding ways to make them alive and meaningful for children through experiences in dance, creative dramatics, music, movies, filmstrips, pictures, or food.

Teachers need to find ways to project the important idea that other people's ways are not "cute" and "quaint" but part of the

[29] *Ibid.*, p. 141.

infinite diversity which human beings have explored in their solutions to problems of social behavior.

**DEVELOPING A FOCUS
FOR THE PROGRAM**

When statements concerning the structure of the disciplines have been sufficiently refined to become the basis for a social studies program, it is possible to visualize how such a program could be developed. The need for unifying and integrative approaches has been underscored by the extent of overlapping and related concerns of the different social science fields.

Various ways of integrating knowledge have been attempted in the history of curriculum development. Science and the social studies programs in the elementary school integrate knowledge into broad fields. The "project" method was another way of integrating knowledge, applying knowledge from a variety of content areas to the solution of life-based programs. The problem posed by any form of integration is to maintain the integrity of the separate fields of inquiry. Since there is much overlapping among the social sciences, both in the questions asked and in the methods used to develop knowledge, it should be possible to integrate them without watering any of the significant elements that delineate these fields. Overarching generalizations applicable to all the social sciences can be expected to develop so that ultimately the teacher's task in integration will be facilitated.

It is essential to have a specific focus for organizing social science ideas for teaching. One method might be to take a single field, such as geography, and develop the social science program around it. The concepts of the related fields would be introduced as they applied to the problem being studied.

Integration by Single-Field Focus

A program of integration around a single field is being developed by a group sponsored by the National Council of Learned Societies and Educational Services, Inc. This program takes its focus from anthropology, although the total program is broader than the social sciences and includes some of the humanities as well. In this program, one can study man and the cultures he has created through anthropology. Geography becomes the vehicle for placing cultures in space and for defining the resources available to the culture. It also helps to understand specific physical limitations and problems that helped to form that culture. History helps to place societies in time. Economics, political science, and other fields are brought to bear in studying the various aspects of culture. The designers of this program, which will run from the kindergarten through the twelfth grade, have organized it so that children begin to deal with "simple" human culture as well as the societies of primates. As the children mature, more complex cultures are studied.[30] The primary grades will study "hunters and gatherers and human evolution."

This program has some important strengths. Its attempt to integrate broad areas of human knowledge must be commended. More integrative efforts of this sort would be useful to teachers. Anthropology is probably one of the more productive choices for a single-field focus for integration. The unity of the total school approach, from kindergarten through high school, promises good articulation and the probability of a spiral curriculum, permitting restudy of the same ideas at more complex levels. The collaboration of academic scholars and educators is a further strength in developing a practical and significant program. Another productive element is the development of fresh source materials for classroom use which increase teachers' abilities to use the program.

This program bears some resemblance to the "recapitulation of the experience of the race" concept that was the basis of curriculum design around 1900. There is similarity in designating some of these earlier cultures as "simple" and assuming that young children will find it easier to understand cultures that are "simpler" than their own. The remoteness of such societies from the lives of American children presents difficult conceptual problems in the beginning grades. Since the proposed new program emphasizes the study of Eskimos, aborigines, and other remote cultures, the children cannot

[30] "Course Content Development in the Social Sciences," *Science Education News*, April 1964, 64(5):1–2, AAAS Misc. Publ.

build learning on prior understanding, nor can they develop learning from first-hand experience, they must use vicarious means of collecting information, exclusively. This is a severe limit upon the range of perceptions available to children. It also requires the total curriculum to be rigidly programmed in order to provide these second-hand experiences. Even though case-study material will be made available to the children, opportunities for learning by discovery will be severely limited.

Programs which ignore children's prior knowledge and experiences in their own culture run counter to well-documented principles about how children learn. When sources for children's first-hand learning are available in such profusion in their own environment, it seems less efficient to study other environments to achieve the goals of the program.

It is possible that weaknesses in this program will be eliminated as it is developed and tested. It provides a clear illustration of how one field in the social sciences can become the focal point for a program to integrate the various social sciences. Such integration maintains the integrity of the separate fields which are taught in a unified way. Programs for young children might similarly be developed in geography, which, having a more observable and physical subject matter, might provide an even better focus for young children's learning.

Geography would be an excellent choice in the kindergarten for a single-field focus for a social studies program because the concreteness of the subject makes it possible for children to experience the raw data from which they can build concepts. Children who have not yet learned to read can learn to use the symbol system which geographers use on maps. Since all the social sciences have geographical elements, this is an important integrating element which can connect different approaches to social science. Geography has the further advantage that it can be a natural bridge between the sciences and the social sciences, which could provide a helpful integrative view of the total kindergarten program. Such a program could be developed around some of the geographic concepts identified by Warman and referred to above.[31]

[31] Henry J. Warman, *op. cit.*, p. 25.

Globalism

A variety of phenomena with which young children have some experience are related to the sphericity of the earth. Time measurements, such as the year, day, hour and minute, and concepts of night and day, are derived from the tempo of rotation and revolution that characterize the movements of the earth. The climate of a region as well as seasonal changes that take place regularly are also related to the shape of the earth and its relationship to the sun. Each of these phenomena can be dealt with in the kindergarten, focusing on these relationships.

Children early become aware of the ways in which time is measured and the need for such measurement. The transition of the child from home to kindergarten helps him become more aware of time, since he is expected to arrive at school at a specified time, and, once there, his pattern of activities is largely regulated by the clock.

The teacher could provide a variety of time measuring devices for children's use and manipulation, including clocks, cooking and egg timers, hourglasses, and the like. Children can use an egg timer to limit turns, when they have to share some desirable toy or equipment. The teacher can make her use of the clock more explicit, perhaps setting a toy clock to show how the real clock's hands will look when play time ends or when it is time to go home. Many other ways to use these time measuring devices are apparent. These devices can be related to the movement of the sun across the sky, for example comparing the position of the sun when the clock indicates it is nine o'clock, with the sun's position at noon. Children can measure the shadow cast by a stick placed in the play yard, and changes can be noted and recorded at different times of day. This simple device can be related to the functional sundial as a more primitive way to measure time.

Such books as *All Kinds of Time*[32] and *Follow the Sunset*[33] can be read to help children further their understandings of the concept of time measurement and its relationship to the movements of the earth and sun. A surprising number of five-year-olds now own their

[32] Harold Behm, *All Kinds of Time*, New York: Harcourt, Brace, 1950.
[33] Herman and Nina Schneider, *Follow the Sunset*, Garden City, N.Y.: Junior Literary Guild and Doubleday, 1952.

own operating wrist watches and are strongly motivated to learn to understand and use them.

The spheroid shape of the earth can be stressed by the use of a beginner's globe in the classroom. The children can easily learn symbols for land, water, and north-south directions and their relationships to the poles. The globe can be used to locate the school and the community, places of birth for foreign-born children, or their parents or grandparents, places which anyone in the class, or an immediate relative or friend has visited, or which is newsworthy and therefore on the children's tongues, or anyplace which anyone in the class finds interesting for any reason.

The teacher might be careful to avoid the misconception that the round globe proves that the earth is round. At a time when there is a lunar eclipse which the children can see, either naturally or on television or in pictures in newspapers or books, the teacher can indicate the ways in which the earth's round shadow is cast upon the moon. Children who live near the coast can be directed to note the dipping horizon as one way to "see" the earth's curvature. Newspaper clippings of pictures of the earth, taken by cameras on satellites which show clearly the earth's curvature, can also be used.

The teacher can use the globe to demonstrate the relationship between the earth and the sun, using a flashlight, for example, to show how the sun illumines part of the globe while the rest is in darkness. Physical models of the earth, sun and moon, in proportion as to size and relative distances from each other are not difficult to make out of different-sized balls, balloons, plaster of Paris over a shaped object, or papier-mâché. Several primary filmstrips, as well as some good children's books, may help to clarify some of these concepts, in addition to the experiences suggested. If the teacher relates movements of the earth and sun to sphericity, she can emphasize some of the concepts of time noted above, especially night and day, the year, and the month.

The changing seasons are often used to provide program ideas in the kindergarten but the plans of teachers and the observable weather and signs of seasonal change do not always mesh. Dealing with seasonal change from the standpoint of concepts of the movements of the earth in relationship to the sun and of the angle of the sun's rays in the different seasons may make more sense to children than some of the more traditional ways. The season's change is related to the global nature of the earth. Weather conditions generally change with the seasons but differ with other geographical factors, but even these can be better understood in relation to globalism.

The round earth on a flat map

While the globe provides an excellent representation of geographic phenomena, representations of the round earth on a flat map can also be introduced. Children can understand that while the globe is a better representation of the shape of the earth than a flat map, maps are essential for detailed studies of areas and for many special purposes. Below are listed five methods by which mapping operations might proceed.

1. *Floor plans.* Children can use doll-house furniture to represent the classroom. This method minimizes symbolization, since miniature tables can represent real ones, and other objects in the classroom may also have their counterparts in miniature, such as chairs, a piano, a sink, and toys. Floor planning should alert the children to spatial relationships within the room, to direction and placement of objects with relation to each other. If any objects are used to represent real objects, symbolization begins with decisions as to which objects represent the real ones in the room, just as map symbols must be chosen. After the children arrange a floor plan with objects, the teacher can draw it on a large piece of newsprint, using heavy black crayon, or using different colored crayons to emphasize different objects represented in the drawing: black for the tables, red for chairs, blue for the piano, brown for utility items such as sink and cupboards, etc. This would be a first effort to relate three-dimensional objects to flat drawings.

2. *Other three-dimensional models.* Children can use unit blocks to construct geographic representations, starting with visible spaces, such as their own classroom or the street right outside the classroom window, so that their representation can be compared with reality while the construction is in process, and afterwards, when the teacher guides the comparison. Concepts of distance, direction, and scale can become problems to solve, so that gradual awareness of the meanings of these concepts can grow. Educational toys such as

Kinder City or *Playschool Village* also provide three-dimensional representational materials, which children can manipulate with ease and pleasure and which they can be encouraged to use occasionally to represent real rather than imaginary places.

3. *Neighborhood maps.* Gradually, flat maps can be introduced, to map the classroom, the school, the school street and the local community. Routes children take to and from school, or on walks to special destinations, can be mapped first by the teacher, and later some children may become interested either in making their own maps or in trying to reconstruct the teacher's maps. In addition, school district maps or teacher-made maps that are traced from county maps, or maps provided by major oil companies, can be used to represent the larger community. Such maps help the child visualize geographic relationships, if he can identify some of the elements represented on the map, such as roads, major intersections, public buildings or parks.

4. *Maps of the United States and the world.* Beginner's maps of the United States and the world, with relatively little detail, can be used by children to locate places and to compare the flat world map with the globe. Children can become aware of the different kinds of geographic representations possible and some of the similarities and differences among them.

5. *Road maps.* Dramatic play may take interesting and unexpected turns if an assortment of road maps and "stop," "go," and other road signs (perhaps those using international symbols) are introduced, preferably with the use of some vehicles, such as bicycles or other wheeled objects that can become pretend busses, cars, or trains. The dramatic play offers children opportunities to play out or practice what they know, elaborate upon it, and develop it in collaboration.

In all these experiences the teacher should stress the concepts of distance, direction, and scale so that children begin to understand the difference between a pictorial representation of an area and a map of the same area.

Areal distinctions; likenesses and differences

As the children learn about their neighborhood and become aware of areal distinctions in their own community, the teacher has an opportunity to make these concepts explicit by showing the children that the local community is organized in its own unique fashion. They can learn that certain areas contain stores while other areas have homes of different kinds. They will also find that some streets are busier than others and that some of these are major routes with bus service. Asking children to find where certain things are in their neighborhood will help them to begin to make areal distinctions. These could be plotted on the map of the neighborhood for the children to see, touch, talk about, and represent in various media, such as clay or paint, if they so desire. If the community contains considerable diversity, such as a waterfront, a rural agricultural area, an industrial area, or a large wholesale market, more vivid distinctions can be made.

Spatial interaction

Because areas are distinct from one another, areal specialization occurs. This can be seen in the difference between a downtown area and a suburb or between an industrial manufacturing area and a shopping center. Growing out of this differentiation is a high degree of interaction between areas. Trade, transportation, communication, and migration are all manifestations of this interaction. The children can begin to see that the dynamic processes of the world are largely interdependent, whether these are economic, sociological, political, or primarily geographic.

Some of this interaction in the form of trade can be observed by children in local stores where selling takes place, as well as in their own homes, where buying needs develop. If children visit a supermarket and notice the places of origin of merchandise, they will find that a great deal comes from distant places. Many of their toys as well as the objects their families use daily have been imported from Europe or the Orient. A tasting party, where children are given small bits of food that come from far away, can help to dramatize the relationship between their daily lives and the larger world upon which so much of their well-being depends. Similarly, displays of toys from distant places will dramatize this conception of spatial interaction, especially when these findings are related to places on maps or globes.

Our nation, often called a nation on wheels, is characterized by travel, migration, and immigration. By plotting on a world map or the globe the places that children have lived or visited, or from which parents or grandparents migrated, this concept of movement of people through space can become personal and meaningful. Children can begin to understand the relationship of geographic areas to each other and the interactions between these areas which have affected their lives.

The interaction of physical forces can also be communicated to kindergarten children in a variety of ways. Young children have seen weather reports on television, and these shows provide an excellent resource for learning about the interaction of physical phenomena. Children can observe weather conditions moving across the country, following the path of a hurricane, a tornado, or a snowstorm as it is reported on these weather shows. Weather maps can be clipped from newspapers and discussed in class. Similar weather maps for children's use can be purchased from equipment companies and used in the classroom.

Perpetual transformation

Change characterizes the lives of children in our culture, almost more than anything else. Children are not usually aware of change as a process but this process can be perceived and experienced if they take short trips from school. In most areas children can observe the destruction or construction of buildings, superhighways and streets and the reconstruction of the centers of cities or the subdivision of farmland for residential purposes.

If the children return frequently to the same site, they can observe the process of change directly, over a period of time. They can watch a project begin, take shape and be completed. Such books as *The Little House*[34] can be read to young children to dramatize the process of change.

An additional resource to provide children with a key to understanding the concept of perpetual transformation are older people in the community. Such persons can be invited into the classroom to talk about the community and how it was different in their youth. Sometimes pictures of realia and artifacts can help make this change more concrete. This approach provides an obvious opportunity to

[34] Virginia Lee Burton, *The Little House*, Boston: Houghton Mifflin, 1942.

integrate historical and geographic concepts, as well as political and other social science concepts.

These and other experiences can be used to help children begin to understand some basic concepts in geography and other social sciences. Correlation with art, music, language arts, and other curriculum areas is easily accomplished. Story books about communities and about people near and far and pictures, songs, and games from far away can extend a child's understanding of the global earth. Constructions in blocks, cardboard cartons, and other materials can be used to represent the concepts as the children work to structure them.

These beginnings can be extended as children move into primary classrooms in which the teachers build programs upon those elements the children have already begun to learn. In this fashion the kindergarten can become the foundation of the entire social studies program in the school system.

Topical Integration

Another way to provide a focus for a social studies program is to select a specific topic for study which can use the concepts and modes of inquiry of each of the fields within the social sciences. The harbor study provided the focus for such topical integration of history and geography concepts. The focus could be determined by a judicious balance of children's interests and the potential fruitfulness of the topic for desired learnings. It would have been possible in each of the two projects described in this book to expand the areas of learning involved in the study.

A study of the harbor, for example, could integrate economic concepts, in addition to concepts from geography and history, highlighting aspects of economic interdependence in the movement of freight and passengers into and out of the harbor. A study of political institutions in local, national, and international politics could be developed. From the anthropologist's point of view, ways in which the American Indian organized himself around water transportation could be studied, comparing functions and problems of the harbor in pre-Colonial days with contemporary problems. These are merely suggestive of how a single topic could be developed as a center for studying selected concepts from the various areas of the social sciences. Developing curriculum content in this way in the social sciences permits meaningful integration of social science concepts. Other advantages of this approach include the teacher's control over the program and the ways in which it can be developed, the ease with which the program can be adapted to the needs and interests of a specific group of children and the wide scope allowed the teacher for selection of learning experiences and inquiries which are direct and first-hand and which make it possible for the child to "discover" meanings.

If such a program is developed, however, the teacher must be careful that the topics covered and the areas studied remain a means to knowledge and not ends in themselves. The topic is only a vehicle for developing knowledge and basic concepts. Facts are learned, therefore, in order to be organized into concepts as well as to advance and illustrate previously learned concepts. If these goals are clearly related to the selection of content, one could even use the traditional topics of the social studies programs for young children, such as, home, school, neighborhood, in such a way that desired concepts are learned. This approach maintains the important advantages of studying an area which is accessible to the children outside of school, which can be explored and perceived in many different situations and which different children may learn from many different experiences.

APPRAISING
NEW PROGRAMS

Several curriculum proposals are now in the process of development for improving the study of social science concepts in the elementary school. Some of these approaches have been described in this chapter, to suggest some of the kinds of programs which can be developed and some of the experiences and materials which may facilitate children's learning. It is becoming increasingly popular to turn out K-12 programs which stress continuity and year-by-year elaboration and development of key concepts. Kindergarten teachers will welcome such programs when the areas assigned for five-year-old learning are related to their abilities and unique ways of learning. Teachers of young children should be vigilant in their appraisal of such programs and should not hesitate to reject those which rely on predominantly second-hand sources and workbook exercises.

BIBLIOGRAPHY

American Council of Learned Societies and the National Council for the Social Studies, *The Social Studies and the Social Sciences*, New York: Harcourt, Brace and World, 1962.

Behm, Harold, *All Kinds of Time*, New York: Harcourt, Brace, 1950.

Burton, Virginia Lee, *The Little House*, Boston: Houghton Mifflin, 1942.

Carpenter, Helen McCraken, *Skill Development in Social Studies*, Thirty-Third Yearbook of the National Council for the Social Studies, 1963.

Darrow, Helen Fisher, *Social Studies for Understanding*, New York: Teachers College Press, Teachers College, Columbia University, 1963.

Elliott, David Loucks, "Curriculum Development and History as a Discipline," unpublished Ed.D. Project, Teachers College, Columbia University, 1963.

Hill, Wilhelmina (Ed.), *Curriculum Guide for Geographic Education*, Norman, Okla.: National Council for Geographic Education, 1963.

Martindale, Don, and Elio D. Monachesi, *Elements of Sociology*, New York: Harper and Brothers, 1951.

National Council for the Social Studies, *Social Studies in Elementary Schools*, Thirty-Second Yearbook, Washington, D.C.: National Education Association, 1962.

National Task Force on Economic Education, *Economic Education in the Schools*, New York: Committee for Economic Development, 1961.

Rose, M. Arnold, *Sociology, the Study of Human Relations*, New York: Alfred A. Knopf, 1957.

Schneider, Herman, and Nina Schneider, *Follow the Sunset*, Garden City, N.Y.: Junior Literary Guild and Doubleday, 1952.

Science Education News, Washington, D.C., American Association for the Advancement of Science, April 1964, 64(5), AAAS Misc. Publ.

Senesh, Lawrence, "The Organic Curriculum: A New Experiment in Economic Education," *The Councilor*, 1960, 21(1).

5

BASIC CONCEPTS IN SCIENCE AND MATHEMATICS

In recent years there has been a shift in the curriculum from a conception of science as things, natural or man-made, or as technology, or as a group of facts about the natural environment. Science is now conceived as a set of facts, a way of looking at physical phenomena and the relationships among them, and a way of describing or explaining these phenomena. Similarly there has been a shift from teaching science as a body of knowledge to teaching science as a mode of inquiry. This change has occurred partly because of the explosion of scientific knowledge, and partly because of the rapid rate at which knowledge is becoming obsolete today.

The necessary shift has been away from fact collecting toward helping children understand the basic processes of science, the ways in which knowledge is developed and the ways in which knowledge is verified. It seems possible to achieve these aims through programs based on the key ideas of science.

SEEKING BASIC CONCEPTS IN SCIENCE

Science education has led the way in pointing to the need to identify the basic organizing ideas as a foundation for the curriculum. Craig, who attempted this task many years ago stated the basic concepts as follows:

1. The universe is very large—*Space*.
2. The earth is very old—*Time*.

3. The universe is constantly changing—*Change*.
4. Life is adapted to the environment—*Adaptation*.
5. There are great variations in the universe—*Variety*.
6. The interdependence of living things—*Interrelationship*.
7. The interaction of forces—*Equilibrium and Balance*.[1]

These conceptions were not to be taught directly to children but were to be used to help organize and interpret the vast array of scientific fact available. Craig gives the following examples of how the concept of change can be approached by children:

Children see water disappear from a dish by evaporation. They pick up rocks which have weathered so much that the rock disintegrates into small pieces in their hands. They see the changes in the sky, in the weather, and in the seasons.
Illustrations of change include such phenomena as rusting of iron, melting of ice, boiling of water, weathering of rocks, variations of weather and of seasons, and innovations produced by man's discoveries and inventions.[2]

The basic concepts identified by Craig provide a framework from which the meaning of such phenomena can be drawn.

Karplus recently stated a different set of concepts to be used as the basis for learning about science.[3] He diagrammed his conceptual scheme as shown on page 96. According to Karplus, when a scientist looks at a phenomenon, he first attempts to identify the real or physical objects that appear to participate in it. These he calls a "system." The scientist may redefine the system later to include more or fewer objects. When there are two or more objects in a system, the scientist examines the relationship between them and how they affect or influence each other. This concept is called "interaction," which the physicist attempts to describe or explain. The interactions observed are explained in terms of more basic interactions, the most basic of which are unexplainable. Observation of interactions of objects within a system, either for description or ex-

[1] Gerald S. Craig, *Science for the Elementary School Teacher*, Boston: Ginn and Co., 1958.
[2] *Ibid.*, p. 96.
[3] Robert Karplus, "One Physicist Looks at Science Education," in A. Harry Passow and Robert R. Leeper (Eds.), *Intellectual Development: Another Look*, Washington, D.C.: Association for Supervision and Curriculum Development, 1964.

planation, is the basic mode of the scientist's work, according to this view. All observations and descriptions lead to comparisons as the next step. If two systems are compared at the same time, they are compared in terms of similarities and differences in properties.

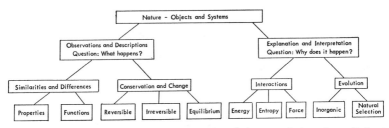

Figure 1. Major Science Concepts. Reproduced, by permission, from Robert Karplus, "One Physicist Looks at Science Education," in A. Harry Passow and Robert R. Leeper (Eds.), *Intellectual Development: Another Look*, Washington, D.C.: The Association for Supervision and Curriculum Development, 1964, p. 93 (Chart 1).

If the same system is compared at different times, one speaks in terms of conservation or change. Evolution accounts for change over long periods of time.[4]

Karplus sees a variety of laboratory experiences as the key to the children's attainment of these basic concepts and a scientific point of view. In the process, children must be provided with experiences that "are different from the usual ones, . . . are based on instruments or devices that may extend the range of the senses," have to do "with unusual environmental conditions," and are "based on the observation of living organisms."[5] Experiences must be provided to help children to become aware of material objects and their properties and to relate objects to other objects. Children are then helped to describe the interaction between objects in a system. This concept of interaction could be illustrated in a tug-of-war, to dramatize the need for interaction to involve at least two objects.[6] Children learn to state both objects in describing an interaction, and to use the proper terms to describe the interactions of various objects in the room.

[4] *Ibid.*, p. 92.
[5] *Ibid.*, p. 86.
[6] *Ibid.*, p. 90.

Children are helped to understand the concept of equilibrium through experiences which show various stages of equilibrium. A melting ice cube, a toy turtle, or a glass of water in which sugar is dissolving can all be described by the concept of equilibrium, and the various states of equilibrium can be disturbed or changed by the children.[7] The glass of sugar water can be stirred. The melted ice cube can be replaced in the freezer, and the toy turtle, which has unwound, can be rewound.

The concept of reversibility and irreversibility can be illustrated through filmed sequences of reversible and irreversible processes.[8] If films are run backwards as well as forwards, children are helped to differentiate between the two processes.

The Science Curriculum Improvement Study at the University of California at Berkeley, of which Robert Karplus is director, has recently published a series of science units derived from his conceptual system. These units, designed for the kindergarten-primary grades, are presently being tested and will probably be revised before their final release. The most basic unit deals with *material objects*. The objective of the unit is "to make the children able to recognize what in their environment are material objects. The objects themselves are to be distinguished from their properties (shape, color, texture, size, etc.), from the influence or effect they have on one another, from the patterns in which they may be arranged, and from the emotions (such as happiness) they arouse." [9] The first of the unit's two chapters contains a series of activities for the kindergarten and first grade that develop the concept of *object* while the second chapter deals with the properties of material objects, including those which do not have definite shape, such as liquids and gases.

The teacher begins the series of lessons by pointing to various objects in the classroom and asking children to tell about them. These objects may include tables, chairs, toys, or any other observable objects. Pictures of things are also used to stimulate the discussion of objects and their attributes. As the children talk about the objects the teacher constantly supports their description of ob-

---

[7] *Ibid.*, p. 94.

[8] *Ibid.*, p. 95.

[9] Science Curriculum Improvement Study, *Teachers Manual for Material Objects* (rev. trial ed.), Berkeley: University of California, 1964, pp. 4–5.

jects in terms of observable attributes rather than in terms of the uses of the objects.

To provide a variety of practice situations, several games are incorporated into the classroom activities. The goal of the games is identification of objects by their attributes. One game includes an "object box," which contains about a half dozen objects. The children are asked to identify an object in the box by the attributes the teacher suggests. Variations on this game are provided to maintain the children's interest and broaden their understandings. Another game suggested is an "object hunt" in which children are sent out to collect objects that have specific attributes. This variation on a scavenger hunt can have children looking for things that are hard, or heavy, or have any other attributes.

The children's concept of object is broadened beyond inanimate objects in the unit through observations of plants and animals. A trip to a zoo, or observation of animals in an aquarium or terrarium is suggested. The attributes of various animals can be observed and compared during these experiences. Similarly a variety of plants are brought into the classroom for observation. This chapter builds upon the observational skills the children learn, to develop groupings based upon observable attributes. The activities suggested include the sorting of buttons by size, shape, and color and the sorting of nuts and washers by their attributes. More complex sorting activities are offered in games that require the sorting and matching of parquetry blocks. Other objects to be sorted include paint chips, bones, and bird seed.

Experimentation with material objects, in the second chapter, is to help teachers . . . "to introduce the concept of *material* by contrasting the specimens which are made of one material with common objects, such as pencils, that are made of several materials." [10] Samples of liquids in jars, including such everyday items as water, honey, liquid starch, cooking oil, and vinegar, are to be studied. Observation and sorting by visual attributes is followed by experiments to establish, as a basis of sorting, their miscibility, that is, their ability to mix with water, and their viscosity, or rate of flow. The children also observe and sort such powdered objects as flour,

---

[10] *Ibid.*, p. 23.

salt, sugar, and powdered milk, and metals and rocks. These objects are described by taste, texture, appearance, and the results of their being mixed with water. Children also study what happens to gases in balloons under varying conditions, recording each observation.

The science program described here can be characterized as a *discovery* approach to science. The content of the course is taught by involving children directly in the processes of science and giving them the opportunity to derive their understanding of science from their own activity. In these units the key elements of science are the concept of *object* and *description and classification of objects by their observable attributes.*

Although a workbook is provided for children in this program, this is far from a workbook approach to science. The workbook is used to help children record their findings during various experiences and to provide additional practice activities. The key to the program is helping children to think like scientists by becoming involved in activities that require scientific behavior and thinking.

Another way of teaching science, of which the chief goal is to teach children elements of scientific method, has recently been developed by the American Association for the Advancement of Science. This program has been a joint undertaking of scientists and teachers and has been developed for the kindergarten and primary grades. The program is based on the assumption that children in the primary grades will derive much benefit from experiences which enable them to acquire certain basic skills and competencies essential to the learning of science. These competencies are listed as:

observation
classification
recognition and use of space/time relationships
recognition and use of numbers and number relations
measurement
communication
inference
prediction[11]

These skills are identified by analyzing what a scientist does when he makes an investigation:

[11] American Association for the Advancement of Science, *Science Education News*, Washington, D.C.: The Association, November 1963, p. 5.

He makes careful observations and measurements. He tabulates and plots his data. He makes calculations. He infers relationships, makes predictions based on his observation, tests these predictions and devises mental models to explain the phenomena he has observed. He communicates his results to others in a variety of ways.[12]

The lessons designed to teach this program contain a statement of the objectives, new vocabulary needed, materials to be used, activities to be offered to the children and evaluation of the lesson. An interesting element in this approach to science is the descriptions of the objectives of the lesson in behavioral terms. This facilitates the teacher's evaluation of the lesson since she is required to determine whether or not the children manifest the behavior described. If they do not manifest this behavior, the lesson is not considered successful. A sample of these behavioral objectives follows:

At the end of this exercise the children should be able to describe the rolling of balls down an inclined plane with particular attention to relative rates of rolling. They should be able to distinguish between a solid and a hollow ball by watching their relative rates of rolling when someone else rolls them down an inclined plane.[13]

This type of evaluation provides the teacher with immediate feedback about the success of her teaching. It also makes evaluation of educational objectives more reliable and measurable.

An experimental edition of the American Association for the Advancement of Science (AAAS) program is at this writing undergoing testing. The first part of the program, which is designed for kindergarten or for first grade in schools which have no kindergarten, deals with concepts of space, observation, number and measurement. The areas covered by the program are alternated throughout the sequences, as follows:[14]

Space

Of the seven units in this program devoted to *space*, the first ones help children to recognize and draw two-dimensional shapes, such

[12] *Ibid.*, p. 2.

[13] American Association for the Advancement of Science, *Science—A Process Approach*, Part II, Washington, D.C.: The Association, 1963, p. 201.

[14] American Association for the Advancement of Science, *Science—A Process Approach*, Part I, Washington, D.C.: The Association, 1963.

as the circle, rectangle, triangle and ellipse, and to recognize these common shapes as components of complex objects and the surfaces of such three-dimensional shapes as the sphere, cube, cylinder, pyramid and cone. Recognition of the fit and arrangement of objects is stressed, as well as the fact that fit applies to function as well as to containment. Children learn to recognize the symmetry of matching pairs in objects and in living things. They learn such directions as up and down, forward and backward, left and right, and to follow such directions as indicated by arrows. Finally, the children begin to deal with concepts of distance and direction.

Number

In the three units of the program devoted to number, children learn to identify sets of objects and to pick out members and properties of sets. Other learning includes distinguishing between sets that have fewer or more members, counting by recognizing sets that differ by one member, ordering sets based upon differences of one member and learning the numerals from zero to ten.

Observation

A broad range of phenomena and objects are covered in the eleven units devoted to skills of observation. Observations include color, shape, size and texture, and from these visual characteristics to sound and odors. Observation of characteristics of leaves and temperature and other weather phenomena follow, in addition to grouping leaves according to their characteristics.

Measurement

Two units devoted to measurement include one on identifying objects of equal length and one on measuring and comparing lengths of objects.[15]

There are many similarities between the science programs described. Each attempts to teach systematically the structure of science. Each is a practical program that could be implemented in the classroom with a minimum of additional materials and equipment. Both provide an adequate structure so that competent

[15] See *Science—A Process Approach*, Part I, supra, for further details.

teachers, with some in-service education, could find them useful. While the content of the two programs overlap, the AAAS program is broader, extending into mathematics.

There are basic differences between these programs, some of which are structural. The Science Curriculum Improvement Study materials permit more flexibility for the teacher. The program suggests areas in which teachers should try to modify the program to meet the specific needs of their own students. The manual admonishes teachers not to expect to tie every lesson into a neat package but to allow loose ends to dangle. The AAAS program, in contrast to this, has a specific set of behavioral goals for each lesson. Teachers are expected to help children in their classes attain these goals before moving on. Evaluation of learnings is based upon children's manifestation of these behaviors. Because this program is so structured, the AAAS curriculum offers less latitude for the modification of the units to meet individual or group differences.

Possibly more basic are differences in the ways these two programs conceive of science. The AAAS program assumes that process is the key to science and therefore it stresses the skills and competencies necessary to participation in the accumulation of scientific evidence. Since one of the attributes of modern science is the quantification of evidence, mathematics is a necessary element in this science program. The SCIS program, on the other hand, views science as a *conceptual scheme*. From this point of view, it is not the collection of objective evidence that is the essence of science, but the act of developing concepts, generalizations and theories. Taking this point of view, this program aims to stimulate children to think about the material world in a scientific way, developing skills of observation and classification because they are required for this purpose.

CHOOSING A
SCIENCE PROGRAM

Either of these two programs offers a far more extensive and significant science program than has been available heretofore. No doubt future science programs will continue to be offered as the fruits of both national and local projects.[16] Each new program will require modification and improvement as the result of experimental work with children. Both programs described above view the child as an active learner, discovering the processes and concepts of science as he participates in scientific activity. Since each program is conceived in terms of a three-or-four-year sequence, decisions as to which to choose may have to rest with school or system supervisors.

Using scientific criteria of parsimony and elegance, one might prefer the Science Curriculum Improvement Study, since it is simpler in form, deals with fewer specific elements, and seems to get at the deeper concerns of science. This, however, is only one of the criteria useful in curriculum selection. A logical choice will also require evidence of the impact of the program on children from a variety of backgrounds, as well as teachers' reactions.

Some scientists have voiced concern that scientific inquiry is too sophisticated and complex for young children to handle without learning incorrect science. They suggest teaching young children scientific content and postponing the study of scientific method for several years. This proposal appears to create a false dichotomy between scientific method and content. Other scientists are equally interested in teaching young children scientific method with little concern for the content since new research and discoveries tend to produce rapid obsolescence of theories and hypotheses.

It is difficult to conceive of an adequate science program which preserves inquiry for mature study and refrains from permeating young children's education with basic elements of scientific inquiry. Much more could be accomplished, it would seem, by working for good scientific attitudes from the beginning, to achieve what Karplus calls "scientific literacy." Teachers could encourage curiosity and cautious and careful observations, help children to note the fallibility of observation and the approximation of measurement, alert them to identify chance elements, and offer opportunities to formulate hunches and devise methods of testing them, as well as experi-

---

[16] Information on new developments in science education is being collected at the Information Clearinghouse on New Science Curricula, a joint project of the American Association for the Advancement of Science and the Science Teaching Center, University of Maryland, College Park, Maryland.

ence the nature of inference and generalization, with attendant errors and bias. Generally, there seems less danger of children's learning incorrect science than of their failure to learn the behavior and practice of scientific modes of inquiry. Surely content and method are so closely interrelated in modern science that one is scarcely understandable without the other.

BASIC CONCEPTS
IN MATHEMATICS

The "new" mathematics does not introduce new systems of quantitative thought. Essentially, the purpose of the "new" approach is to teach children to look for, and find, quantitative meanings, relationships, and patterns. This is a significant change from past teaching goals which chiefly stressed rote memorization and mechanical, computational skills, which are singularly inappropriate for young children's learning. Because mathematics is now being taught to emphasize the child's discovery of meaning in his quantitative universe, it has become a discipline well suited to the growing needs of five-year-olds.

Mathematics, one of the oldest and most highly organized of all the disciplines, offers an excellent example of the possibilities inherent in the collaboration of scholars and educators for more productive teaching. Several programs have already been developed in mathematics. As would be expected, there is greater agreement among the mathematicians as to what beginning concepts should be taught, than in most other fields, but there is lack of unanimity even here.

In general, new programs in elementary school mathematics include a wider range of mathematical concepts than in the past and these ideas and relationships are pursued in greater depth. The language of mathematicians is used in most new programs so that concepts and vocabulary are learned together. While "set" is a basic, undefined term in mathematics, the new programs introduce set theory, usually defining sets as well-defined collections. The Twenty-ninth Yearbook of the National Council of Teachers of Mathematics offers a detailed overview of the topics and concepts now being introduced in elementary school, from sets to number sentences.[17] For example, under "sets," such concepts are included as set equality and subsets, universal sets, Venn diagrams, ordered sets, and finite and infinite sets. This approach invariably includes such concepts as cardinality, numeration, ordered pairs, mathematical symbol systems, and such set operations as union, intersection, and separation.

Some mathematical concepts now being introduced into the early grades of school include nondecimal number bases, geometric relationships concerning points, lines, and planes, and some elementary forms of symbolic logic and topology. Researchers have been trying to find concrete ways to represent many abstract patterns and relationships which it was formerly assumed could not be so represented for young children's learning.

Very few mathematics programs are available at the kindergarten level. Of these, the Greater Cleveland Mathematics Program is commercially available through Science Research Associates, while the Minnesota Mathematics Program, part of its Minnemast Project, is one of several available only on an experimental basis. Other programs are becoming available as individual researchers on various campuses complete experimental projects and offer programs to teachers, either on a sequential basis or as "enrichment" for a variety of grade levels.

The Greater Cleveland Program represents a listing of beginning concepts in set theory and consists of a logical sequence of ideas from the point of view of the mathematician. These concepts are developed in an accompanying workbook and teacher's guide which are similar to the materials teachers are accustomed to working with in basal reader series. In addition, there is a separate booklet which lists the key concepts through the primary grades.[18] Thus, teachers are free to use only the statement of key concepts on which to build their own programs, to use the ready-made programs which have been prepared, or to adapt these to their own purposes. There are

[17] National Council of Teachers of Mathematics, *Topics in Mathematics for Elementary School Teachers*, Twenty-Ninth Yearbook, Washington, D.C.: The Council, 1964, pp. 6–18.

[18] Educational Research Council of Greater Cleveland, *Key Topics in Mathematics for the Primary Teacher*, Chicago: Science Research Associates, 1961.

several other programs for the kindergarten and primary grades which initiate the study of sets and the language of set theory in the kindergarten, as for example, *Sets and Numbers,*[19] a Stanford University project published by Singer.

CHARACTERISTICS OF NEW MATHEMATICS PROGRAMS

There are many advantages to these new approaches to mathematics. The new goals of understanding and enjoying mathematics constitute a significant change which offers bright prospects to children in learning a subject which has traditionally been regarded with distaste. Opportunities for learning by discovery are now possible for almost any mathematics concepts. Possibilities are widened for open-ended learning and the elimination of arbitrary limits on what children can learn.

Teachers will particularly welcome statements of key concepts, which offer a concise listing of beginning ideas in mathematics in terms of meanings and relationships. Teachers' guides and manuals can also be of considerable help to new teachers and to those unfamiliar with the new approach. Much fresh material can be found in these guides, to be used as reference sources.

Along with much that is positive in these new approaches to mathematics can be found some elements of doubtful value. Much of the criticism revolves around the lack of relationship between the teaching styles of the programs and the learning styles of young children. Assumptions are made about children's prior experiences and previously learned skills, such as making generalizations or differentiating between categories, which may not be valid. Poor choices of learning materials and situations often create blocks to learning those concepts that could easily be found embedded in familiar material and situations. The emphasis in some programs on precise verbal forms of complicated concepts rather than meanings may create a block for the child who is learning as well as for the teacher who may perceive these requirements as unreasonable expectations.

[19] Patrick Suppes, *Sets and Numbers*, Books 1 and 2, Syracuse, N.Y.: Singer, 1963 and 1964.

Far too many of the programs consist of formal, total-class learning experiences and work with workbooks. Such an approach limits the teacher's ability to meet individual differences in the classroom through individual or small group activities. The opportunities for discovery of concepts by children are also limited by the lack of imaginative suggestions, despite the fact that "discovery" is emphasized in the programs. Elements of disguised drill, often in the form of games, can also lead to a dislike of the materials due to boredom and fatigue. Some of the games utilize competitive techniques which reward the "champion" who wins. It is not clear how this type of teaching will motivate all five-year-olds to continue to try to learn, when inevitably the same one or two children will always win.

Perhaps the major weakness of some new programs may be their undervaluing of teaching methodology. An implicit assumption in such programs is that methodology flows directly from the concepts to be learned, as though the nature of the learner is irrelevant. Yet teachers who try to reach children from different backgrounds with varying abilities and styles of learning are sharply aware of the need for many methodologies as well as variety in materials and equipment. Even though teachers' guides contain suggestions for alternatives and variations, their essentially prescriptive nature tends to limit teaching efforts to the steps which are detailed. This poses a danger to the development of creative teaching. A greater danger may be that teachers who find the guides are not well adapted for young children will be likely to refuse to teach the concepts in any form, concluding that the ideas are unsuitable to young children. It will be unfortunate if good new curriculum material is to be discarded because of poor methodology. Good programs can only grow out of respect for and understanding of how young children learn.

Deans raises some fundamental questions of concern regarding experimental mathematics programs. One of her concerns is whether all the content that can be taught to young children should be taught; that is, the criteria to be used for judging what should be taught in mathematics. She suggests that we must ask whether a specific body of content represents the best expenditure of a child's time in his mathematical growth and general intellectual development. She questions the appropriateness of the content of new mathematics programs for children who are not gifted. Other concerns deal with the provision for the sequential development of new mathematics concepts after they are introduced and the possibility of the fusion of ideas from experimental programs into regular programs. In-service training for teachers in new programs is another problem.[20]

Deans also raises the problems of formalism, the introduction of precise language to young children, and the tendency of newer programs to minimize application of mathematics. Adult mathematicians, eager to accelerate the young child's mathematical development, sometimes lose sight of the child's need for nonsedentary, active, self-propelled learning situations. These mathematicians prefer to use imitation and drill, repetitive workbook exercises, and other procedures which are likely to be boring and unattractive to young children, few of whom score 150 or above in IQ tests. Practice situations can, however, stimulate considerable interest among young children, if they can be embedded in application activities which are meaningful, whether in scoring games, counting to obtain needed sums, using units of measurement for purposeful activities, or any other of the innumerable opportunities which abound in good kindergarten programs.

SEQUENCE OF CONCEPTS

The mathematicians who have developed the new programs have stressed the logical, sequential character of mathematics. They have also stressed the need to teach mathematics in a well-defined sequence, so that, for example, teaching sets of five follows sets of four and subtraction follows addition operations. While no solid research supports the need to teach in sequence in order that the sequential character of the discipline be understood, the sheer logic of the position tends to support this assumption.

In the report of an experimental mathematics program in a Pennsylvania elementary school, it was suggested that instead of following a rigid sequence in teaching the various arithmetic operations, per-

---

[20] Edwina Deans, *Elementary School Mathematics*, Washington, D.C.: Department of Health, Education, and Welfare, U.S. Government Printing Office, 1963, pp. 98–100.

mitting children to study all of them simultaneously was helpful to children's understanding of the relationships involved.[21] This study suggests that there need be no parallel between the sequence in which mathematics concepts are taught and the logical way they are ordered in set theory.

Dienes is also critical of the logical approach to developing learning sequences in mathematics in the early school years. He points out that, "Logic consists in reflecting on how this and other structures function and I find it difficult to see how it is possible to reflect on something that is not yet there." [22] Like the Rasmussens, he stresses the need for children to play freely with many types of concrete materials so that explorations can lead to discovery of meaning and interrelationships, which teachers can help children to stabilize. He recommends such materials as his own "multi-base" blocks, or other systematic mathematics materials.

Programs must be based on what children know. Before new programs are instituted in the classroom, teachers need to appraise the skills and understandings which children have. This can be done individually and informally in the early months of the school year. Teachers can ascertain children's abilities in rational and rote counting, grouping, identifying geometric shapes, recognizing numeral names and symbols, differentiating between cardinal and ordinal numbers, making size and number comparisons, and other such basic, beginning concepts.

Having determined what prior learnings children have when school begins, teachers are equipped to select beginning concepts and vary the teaching methods and content to the needs of the children in the group. Formulations of key concepts can help teachers to focus sharply on conceptual learning, combine manipulative and verbal learning, and to provide a wealth of supplemental and reinforcing activities so that a variety of meaningful practice activities can be initiated.

As more mathematicians learn more about young children and how they learn and grow, and more teachers learn more about

---

[21] Don and Lore Rasmussen, "The Miquon Mathematics Program," *The Arithmetic Teacher*, 1962, 9(4):180–187.

[22] Zolton P. Dienes, *Building Up Mathematics*, London: Hutchinson Educational, 1960, p. 11.

mathematical concepts, the school curriculum in mathematics is bound to improve in quality and results.

SOCIAL EXPERIENCES
IN DEVELOPING
MATHEMATICS CONCEPTS

Many kindergarten programs have excellent opportunities for exploration and learning of quantitative concepts in various types of social experiences. Many teachers are alert to these learning situations and regularly develop the mathematical content inherent in them.

For example, fairly routine situations include matching crayon boxes to children, or drinking straws to milk containers or cookies, paper napkins, paper cups or other table utensils to children. Counting money, noting coin equivalences, and making change are usual attributes of the money collections for milk, Red Cross, bus trips, and book fairs. Some teachers initiate activities which stimulate quantitative learning or problem solving, through measurement at the carpentry table or in cooking experiences, or counting or grouping with dominoes, blocks, cubes, beads, pegs, or other concrete, manipulable objects.

The new programs tend to overlook the many excellent opportunities for learning mathematics concepts in children's first-hand social experiences in the classroom. This may be a reaction to "incidental" mathematics learning. Scholars are trying to insure that the focus on the mathematics involved cannot be overlooked, by removing them from purely social situations. It would seem to be more fruitful to redirect teachers to abstract and emphasize mathematics learnings wherever they occur. It is also sound to build children's learnings inductively from their own experiences. In many classrooms, the teacher will find that her main mathematics goal must be to create mathematical experiences from which the most primitive and basic number understandings grow. If good practice situations can then be developed to help children stabilize such learnings, children can be expected not only to learn the new mathematics concepts but also find more pleasure in the learning.

SOME SUGGESTIONS
FOR PRACTICING
MATHEMATICS

In lieu of workbook drill, kindergarten children can spend time profitably solving mathematical problems and practicing some mathematics understandings. Kindergarten teachers can begin to analyze their school day to find opportunities for this within existing programs. Milk money or other money collections can provide such opportunities to practice rational counting, work with cardinal numbers, grouping within ten, and learning money denominations and equivalents. Beginning addition and subtraction operations may also be provided by this routine activity. Other routine tasks can similarly provide learning opportunities as children assume responsibility for taking attendance and distributing supplies or snacks.

Play money can be introduced into the kindergarten to provide mathematical learnings within spontaneous play. Blocks and other physical objects can also provide play-based mathematical experiences. A more systematic approach to making mathematical discoveries can include using such materials as the Stern Structured Mathematics materials, the Cuisenaire rods, the Montessori beads and rods, and other similar materials that are available from various educational equipment companies.

Children can make quantitative comparisons as part of such activities as cooking, carpentry, block building, and sewing. They can use these activities to learn and practice such concepts as longer, thicker, heavier, or wider. Informal comparisons can lead to more formal measurement concepts through the use of clocks, egg timers, simple rulers, balances, scales, and thermometers. Children can learn to keep score in their games or to keep track of turns taken through the use of physical objects, such as blocks or beads, or by using chalk or crayon tallies. Teachers can help children learn a variety of ways of keeping quantitative records in science projects as well as in other areas of the program. Such simple records would allow the children to make comparisons over a period of time.

Teachers can be as systematic in rotating mathematical tasks among the children in the class as they are in assigning "helper" tasks. Teachers can also find systematic ways to observe and record each child's progress so that guidance can be individual and precise instead of general and global. Unnecessary drill can be dispensed with but, when the teacher finds some basic common confusions or misunderstandings, she can structure a learning situation which can offer needed practice opportunities to the whole group under her supervision. This is the time for "games" and verbalizing processes of thinking, to shape, stabilize, and clarify developing concepts.

The block corner is an ideal area to stimulate learning some geometric concepts but many other materials contribute to such learnings, including woodworking, work with various art media, and a variety of practical problems. Names are always useful and the teacher can be alert to identify triangles, rectangles, circles, squares, and other common geometric shapes, and to encourage children to identify and use the names correctly.

BRIDGES TO ABSTRACT THINKING

Most teachers are clear about teaching based on very specific and concrete experiences, or purely abstract ones. The most difficult kind of teaching is finding ways to bridge the gap between learning which is very concrete and the abstract meanings which must ultimately be grasped.

It is sometimes assumed that if children have enough concrete experiences of a particular type, the discovery of the generalities involved will dawn upon them by the sheer weight of the experiences they have piled up. Mathematics teachers are frequently made sharply aware of the weaknesses of this assumption. For example, there are many games which children play, such as Tic-Tac-Toe, in which most children never discover the winning strategy, although they should, if sheer multiplicity of experience were to accomplish this.

Strategies of playing games, and of inductive thinking, could be important learning situations for children if teachers could find appropriate guidance techniques which could alert children to the fact that there are strategies, that some are more efficient for some purposes than others, and that these may be tested in specific cases. Guided games may be helpful where the purpose is not to find the "champion" but to focus on which strategies help and which do not. This shifts the spotlight to the various strategies which are possible, to observing and recording which ones are used and which ones are better than others. The teacher might set up teams to try out some different strategies, note results, compare them, and then try to draw some conclusions about their efficiency. Teachers' roles should include helping children to analyze possibilities, to know that there are usually more possibilities than appear at first sight, and to value different ways to test hunches. Children can be introduced to checkers and even chess, both of which help them become aware of the variety of opening moves and their chances for success.

In the study of economic concepts, the focus on family size and variation led to some symbolic and abstract ways of patterning quantitative data. The problem was to make the child conscious of his own family size and composition, of its difference from and similarity to other families, and of the distribution of different kinds of families within the class population. A bar graph was selected as a simple and popular way of symbolizing economic data.

Children were made aware of the size and composition of their own families through class discussions, in which the definition of "family" was developed through many specific instances. The need to record this information in some fashion was suggested in a variety of ways. Methods of recording and preserving the quantitative information included having the children sort themselves into groups, representing different kinds of families, tallying frequencies on a chalkboard, having children each place a block "instead of himself" in the correct group, and using construction paper figures to represent the specific family groups listed. The data was transferred to a flannel board with further abstraction when each child placed a flannel representation of a block "instead of a real block instead of himself," and finally the same data was transformed into the further abstraction of a bar graph. The graph was readily understood as carrying the same meaning as the flannel board, the block substitution, and the physical grouping of the children themselves.

Thus a bridge was slowly built between the children's completely concrete experiences and the abstract symbolism which was patterned to represent well-understood quantities. An important feature of this gradual accretion of meaning appeared to be the substantial block of time allocated to developing these concepts, a period of two-and-a-half months, as well as the repetition of most of the process at the end of the period. The repetition brought satisfaction to the children when they recognized the materials and the concepts involved. It contributed to further clarification as well, as the children used and verbalized these meanings.

Teaching methods by which the children were guided to develop these understandings included:

1. The development of clear statements of behavioral outcomes for planned learning experiences.
2. The development of appropriate testing devices to gauge the distribution of learnings in the group and to plan for further learning activities.
3. The teacher's willingness to raise the ceiling on her expectations of children.
4. The planning of a variety of sensory stimuli.
5. The selection of dramatic and active ways of representing ideas, and the "reality" testing of children's concepts.
6. "Revisiting" ideas after a substantial lapse of time to correct and reinforce growing understanding and to stabilize it.
7. Considerable discussion and introduction and use of appropriate language along with all the experiences introduced.
8. Generous use of audio-visual materials designed to help expand meanings.
9. Free manipulation of appropriate materials for experimentation and discovery.
10. Planned and systematic teacher guidance of the learning activities toward preselected behavioral outcomes.

Perhaps an essential ingredient in the above methodologies was the stimulation of a problem-solving attitude toward quantitative material, in a noncompetitive atmosphere of pleasure and satisfaction in acquiring new understandings.

Abstract thinking grows out of understandings derived from concrete experiences but thinking must be molded gradually to take increasingly general form. The teacher must be conscious of working toward generalization, linking each concrete experience with some abstract element, helping children to verbalize and express the ideas they are learning. The unfamiliar elements are gradually introduced, building toward their inclusion in a higher order of understanding. Thus the teacher helps children to build a bridge between the world of concrete experiences and the abstract ways of representing it.

BIBLIOGRAPHY

American Association for the Advancement of Science, *Science Education News*, Washington, D.C.: November 1963.

————, *Science—A Process Approach*, Parts I and II. Washington, D.C.: The Association, 1963.

Banks, J. Houston, *Learning and Teaching Arithmetic*, Boston: Allyn and Bacon, 1964.

Craig, Gerald S., *Science for the Elementary School Teacher*, Boston: Ginn and Co., 1958.

Deans, Edwina, *Elementary School Mathematics*, Washington, D.C.: Department of Health, Education, and Welfare, U.S. Government Printing Office, 1963.

Dienes, Zolton P., *Building Up Mathematics*, London: Hutchinson Educational, 1960.

Educational Research Council of Greater Cleveland, *Key Topics in Mathematics for the Primary Teacher*, Chicago: Science Research Associates, 1961.

Hightower, Robert, and Lore Rasmussen, *First-Grade Diary*. Chicago: Mathematics Laboratory Materials, Learning Materials, 1964.

Karplus, Robert, "Beginning a Study in Elementary School Science," *American Journal of Physics*, 1962, 30:1–9.

————, "The Science Curriculum—One Approach," *The Elementary School Journal*, February 1962, 62:243–252.

National Council of Teachers of Mathematics, *Topics in Mathematics for Elementary School Teachers*, Twenty-Ninth Yearbook, Washington, D.C.: The Council, 1964.

Passow, A. Harry, and Robert R. Leeper (Eds.), *Intellectual Development: Another Look*, Washington, D.C.: Association for Supervision and Curriculum Development, 1964. (Pp. 59–98, Papers by J. Richard Suchman and Robert Karplus.)

Rasmussen, Don, and Lore Rasmussen, "The Miquon Mathematics Program," *The Arithmetic Teacher*, 1962, 9(4):180–187.

Science Curriculum Improvement Study, *Teachers Manual for Material Objects* (rev. trial ed.), Berkeley: University of California, 1964.

6

ROLE OF THE
KINDERGARTEN
TEACHER

Kindergarten teachers who focus on conceptual development will recognize their responsibility to provide appropriate and challenging experiences to extend and develop children's understandings. They will be actively introducing and initiating new experiences for children as well as supporting and extending activities which emerge from the routine activities of the kindergarten day. The role teachers play will be different from the traditional conception of the kindergarten teacher.

It is not uncommon to hear that the only significant characteristic of a kindergarten teacher is a warm and accepting personality. Carried to its logical conclusion, this point of view would make the teacher nothing more than a highly paid "baby sitter." However, educational logic points to the teacher's *doing* as well as *being*.

Implicit in education is the assumption that there are ways in which the teacher teaches which can result in children's learnings. This implicit assumption is often disregarded. The tendency is to concentrate *not* on what teachers do to advance teaching and learning but only on the learning process itself. This is not always helpful since it is difficult to see what implications this has for teaching. There is, in fact, little practical application in the classroom to be derived from learning theory as presently constituted.

Bruner suggests that a theory of instruction is needed, concerned with the relationship between how things are presented and how they are learned.[1] Such a theory, he says, should be constructed around

---

[1] Jerome S. Bruner, "Needed: A Theory of Instruction," *Educational Leadership*, 1963, 20:524.

four problems: predisposition to learn effectively; optimal structuring of knowledge for economy, productiveness, and power; optimal sequence; and the nature and pacing of rewards and punishments.[2] A recent study by Taba is a provocative effort to study the impact of teaching strategies on the development of thinking.[3] Taba's study suggests that efficient teaching strategies can help lower-IQ children make as much progress as their higher-IQ classmates.

Lacking a carefully developed theory of instruction, it is necessary to view teaching practices pragmatically and to recommend those which have been and promise to continue to be productive in concept development. Bruner's concern for the learner's "predisposition to learn effectively" is translated here to mean *teaching* for effective predisposition to learn. This chapter is mainly concerned with just this, how teaching practices can enhance and stimulate the predisposition to learn.

PLANNING

The teacher who waits for things to happen is at the mercy of fate. If the teacher is willing to plan, she can insure that certain events will occur. She is also prepared to guide the children's observations and perceptions and to help them to organize the information they collect.

"Units," which have been popular for a long time, may not always be the most productive forms in which to plan for children's learnings. Many kindergarten teachers feature a succession of units, often of a week's duration each, with one topic quickly succeeding another. Unit topics or themes are often too big, broad, and complex for such rapid treatment. Instead, it is suggested that goals for five-year-olds be conceived of as worthwhile learnings which take considerable periods of time to attain, not one or two weeks.

Effective planning starts with long-range goals. From these develop immediate and short-range goals and the experiences most likely to result in progress toward the desired learning. This type of planning enables the teacher to chart possible accomplishments

[2] *Ibid.*, pp. 524–525.

[3] Hilda Taba (Director), *Thinking in Elementary School Children*, San Francisco: San Francisco State College, 1964.

and to review regularly the goals toward which she is working. Relating her daily planning to her long-range goals must become the teacher's continuous, conscious procedure.

Long-Range Goals

It is the long-range goals which are the yardstick of the value of any program. They provide the base for testing the significance of daily and weekly planning for children. Plans which enable children to move toward the behavior and understandings defined as long-range goals are productive.

Long-range goals may be stated as specific behavioral outcomes in a number of areas such as social learnings or physical skills and in such content areas as language arts, science, mathematics or social studies. For example, behavioral outcomes in language arts may be some of the following:

1. ability to understand and to follow directions
2. ability to communicate with other children and adults
3. ability to tell a well-known story in sequence
4. ability to converse in sentences
5. ability to use good, colloquial, English speech
6. ability to articulate and enunciate sounds clearly
7. ability to pronounce words properly
8. ability to listen for brief periods to other children and adults

This is not meant to be an exhaustive list, but simply to suggest the characteristics of a behavioral definition of goals.

In science, mathematics, and social studies, behavioral goals could be developed from the basic concepts or the "big ideas" as suggested in Chapters 4 and 5. For example, in mathematics, the decimal base of the number system is one of the fundamental concepts to be learned. This concept might be stated in terms of the behavioral goal of counting or grouping to ten and combining tens. Beginnings can be made in developing this concept in the kindergarten through such activities as taking attendance, distributing milk and cookies or crayons and paper, or in other ways. A teacher is not likely to guide children to group by tens, unless she is consciously working to help the class become aware of this mathematical idea. Without this goal, she is likely to guide the class to count everything in units, no matter what the sum is likely to be.

When the long-range goals have been clearly stated, the teacher plans specific activities, experiences and instructional materials which will carry as many of the children in the class as far as possible toward the attainment of these goals.

Short-Range Plans

Specific short-range plans should be realistic and appropriate for specific children. Plans must be tailored to the needs, abilities and prior experiences of children. Immediate plans are needed to help children move forward in small steps toward selected goals. Planning for children who come from disadvantaged backgrounds must be different from planning for children who come from privileged homes.

Planning, then, looks first toward stated long-range goals and then toward immediate, small steps in the desired direction. When progress is too slow, analysis is needed to isolate the deficiencies and to construct better plans. Milner points out that a plan for teaching is a guide for action, that it constitutes a service tool for flexible use and for "on-the-spot" changing as needed.[4]

The extent of detail in planning depends upon the personality and experience of the teacher. Some teachers are more secure if all details are preplanned while others enjoy the challenge of some improvisation. New teachers need very detailed planning because they have yet to build the repertoire from which they will ultimately be able to improvise.

Short-range plans, which challenge the ingenuity of the teacher, offer many different paths to the same desired conceptual learning. Which one to choose, how directly to move, at what pace for different children—all these factors must be weighed in making selections. There are few blueprints available to the teacher searching for optimum vehicles of learning. A willingness to experiment, change and evaluate each experience is the essential ingredient to

[4] Ernest J. Milner, *You and Your Student Teacher*, New York: Teachers College Press, Teachers College, Columbia University, 1954, pp. 27–32.

successful short-range planning for young children. As experience accumulates and is replicated by many teachers, more guidelines will be available to the teachers of tomorrow's kindergarten children.

TEACHING FOR DISCOVERY

Helping children gain the skill for seeking, self-direction, self-selection and discovery of meaning is teaching children to form life-long habits of disciplined learning. If students are accustomed to being "told" what they should know, all through their formative years, they will scarcely emerge as logical, reasoning adults. Five-year-olds are not too young to take first steps in this direction.

Bruner has contributed some helpful analysis of the characteristics and benefits of acts of discovery in learning. He notes that discovery

. . . is in its essence a matter of rearranging or transforming evidence in such a way that one is enabled to go beyond the evidence so reassembled to new insights. It may well be that an additional fact or shred of evidence makes this larger transformation possible. But it is often not even dependent on new information.[5]

In addition, Bruner notes that discovery favors the well-prepared mind, one which is either expecting that there will be patterns or meanings to be found or which is expecting to devise ways of fruitful seeking. It is possible, he points out, to discover things and not know it.

Benefits of learning by discovery are stated by Bruner as increasing intellectual potency, shifting from extrinsic to intrinsic rewards, learning the heuristics of discovery, and providing an aid to conserving memory.[6] Thus Bruner proposes that children who learn by discovery techniques may be better prepared to know what they have learned, to transform this learning into new insights and higher order abstractions or generalizations and to learn the satisfactions of learning for the reward of discovery instead of for external rewards and punishments. In addition, in learning the heuristics or methods of discovery, he may learn a style or technique of problem

[5] Jerome S. Bruner, *On Knowing*, Cambridge, Mass.: Belknap Press of Harvard University Press, 1962, pp. 82–83.

[6] *Ibid.*, p. 93.

solving or inquiry which will serve him in almost any problem he encounters. Finally, reducing complexity in terms of "a person's own interests and cognitive structures," Bruner says, makes it most accessible to memory and future use.[7]

Bruner and Vygotsky both cite the child's dialogues with the parent as beginning the process of thought development. So does the teacher initiate thinking along selected lines by her dialogues with individual children, or small groups in the class. The teacher who encourages the child to participate actively in such dialogues moves him to experiment in manipulation. The teacher helps children to formulate hypotheses, to carry out experimental activities to test such hypotheses and finally to evaluate the findings in terms of the hypotheses made. When the child is able to internalize such thinking, carrying it through unaided by the teacher, the beginning of autonomous thinking begins, Bruner says.

An example of the way children develop hypotheses occurred on the second day of the geography–history study. The children had taken a trip to the river to see the boats. They were able to look down the river and were fortunate to catch the *Queen Mary* as it began to dock. They could observe tugboats coming out to assist the ocean liner in this difficult maneuver.

In a later discussion of the trip, several of the children remarked about the tugs coming out to the *Queen Mary*. The children were asked if they knew why the tugs were going to the ocean liner's assistance, and their replies were:

"To push it," said Sandy.
The researcher asked, "Why would the tugboat push the ship?"
"Maybe the *Queen Mary* didn't have an engine," responded Jerry.
"If the tugboat is pushing it, does that mean it doesn't have an engine?" the researcher countered.
Lucy replied, "Maybe the battery is dead."
"Maybe it broke." "Maybe it ran out of gas." "Or it's stuck," replied some other children.
"Those are good ideas," said the researcher. "When you run out of gasoline in a car, or the battery is dead, sometimes another car has to push you. Does anyone have any other ideas why the tugboat would be pushing or pulling the big ocean liner?"
Randy responded, " 'Cause it can't go into shore too well."

[7] *Ibid.*, p. 90.

"Why not, Randy?" asked the researcher.

"Because it's too big and it can't see far down."

Jerry added, "Sometimes there is so much ice that they can't go through, so then the tugboats come."

Had this been a group of adults, many of the ideas would seem far-fetched and even ludicrous. But the conjectures of these five-year-olds provided the beginnings of hypothesis development. The children used their experiences with auto travel to attempt to explain a new phenomenon. Running out of gas and having a dead battery in a car are all-too-familiar occurrences in our automobile-oriented lives. Similarly, the remarks about the ice and the *Queen Mary* having no engine also had their origins in the children's experiences. There was ice floating in the river at this time of year, and the sight of tugboats pulling barges down the river was a familiar one. The idea that the boat needed the help of tugs because it was so large, the most nearly correct explanation, was picked up by other children in the class to explain similar occurrences in later experiences. The recognition of the appropriateness of this explanation in similar situations indicated there was sufficient understanding of this concept for correct application.

If the teacher is to reap the benefits of teaching for discovery, she must want children to develop ways of collecting and marshaling facts so that ideas, understandings, and principles emerge. Her teaching ought to be sufficiently open-ended so that any achievements are theoretically possible. Children who have previously reached higher achievement levels may be able to tackle the same problems and ideas as the rest of the class at more complex or abstract levels or in greater depth. Teaching for key concepts permits the teacher to develop the same focus for all children, but requires her to vary the conditions for learning for different children.

TEACHING MOTIVATION

A significant element in the predisposition to learn is the motivation of the learner. Psychologists have stressed the cognitive hungers and drives to learn that are so intense in the young child. Basically, the normal child can be expected to bring considerable motivation to any learning situation which is appropriate to his developmental level. However, this strong motive to learn can be weakened or strengthened, depending upon the child's experiences in learning. A teacher who assumes that teaching must be limited to the narrow confines of motivation which the uneducated child brings to school is unaware of the exciting possibilities which exist in helping children develop new and more complex interests.

When the teacher realizes she can "teach" motivation, she can emphasize and reinforce motives which are desirable and necessary for learning. "Motivating" children is therefore a prime factor teachers include in their planning. Teachers know that children's motivation can be reinforced and guided to learning goals which expand and grow in harmony with the child's own development.

It is often assumed that teacher's efforts to "motivate" or stimulate young children's interests must be limited to making materials available and noting the results. Yet children's apparent lack of "motivation" to use new materials or to use well-known materials in new ways may be simply due to their lack of information or experience. Fruitful use of materials or experiences may result when children become aware of even fairly obvious possibilities. Helping to "motivate" children can include such diverse teacher activities as calling children's attention to some little-noticed object, focusing in greater detail on something so that perceptions become clearer, talking with children to help them become aware of their own knowledge or making suggestions for exploring the possibilities of materials.

In the economics study, the children failed to perceive any possibilities for store play when the store counter, empty food cartons, and other props were first introduced into the classroom. Left to themselves, the children might never have developed the store game. It was the teacher's suggestions, in very specific terms, which helped to launch the store play initially. Once store play was started, it was possible to revive flagging interest at intervals by adding new props or suggesting additional dimensions to the play through related experiences.

Motivating Use of Art Materials

Most young children enjoy easel painting and find satisfaction in this medium. But many children tire of painting after a while, without having made much progress in their skills, abilities, perceptions, or standards of performance.[8] An example of a teacher motivating children to more skillful performance follows:

> A teacher of five-year-olds deplored the lack of progress in easel painting in her classroom in the second half of the year. The children seemed to be in a rut, painting the same patterns or pictures daily. One day, the teacher began to talk to the group about their families, asking children to list individually the members of their families. Soon after this, the teacher asked some of the children whether they would like to paint "family portraits." Some children seized on this suggestion at once, and the class was soon completely caught up in a new trend of painting pictures of members of one's family. The teacher's suggestion impelled some of the children into the problems of how to represent human forms and how to show size and other relationships. The children began to ask more advanced questions and they could be impelled to observe or perceive more purposefully and in greater detail than before. As soon as children make a problem their own, purposeful inquiry becomes possible, which was impossible before that.

Motivating Use of Blocks

In the geography–history study, children were motivated to use blocks in new ways when it was suggested that they construct waterfront facilities with blocks, after a number of first-hand experiences in exploring New York City's waterfront facilities. A long strip of blue shelf paper was taped to the floor to represent the Hudson River. The suggestion was made that the children build the waterfront. Over a period of several days, the block building continued with progressively greater elaboration as children added bridges, wharves, and other buildings. Similarly, after walking through the neighborhood and mapping it, the children were provided with a grid of black paper pasted to the floor that encouraged them to represent the familiar buildings in the neighborhood with blocks, placing these "buildings" along the paper streets in the proper relationship to one another. As in the example with easel painting, a familiar material which had been in frequent classroom use was made the vehicle of ideational progress. Simply adding

[8] For more detail on motivating art work, see Blanche Jefferson, *Teaching Art to Children*, Boston: Allyn and Bacon, 1959.

a strip of paper to represent the river gave children new grist for their mill.

In many classrooms where block construction becomes stale and unprofitable, the teacher plans for neighborhood trips to an airport, to the firehouse or post office, or to the local shopping center. This often provides the children with the new ideas and observations they need for fresh inspiration. If the teacher works with the children to relate their observations to some basic ideas, the new play may develop faster, further and more meaningfully.

Block play need not be the limited, repetitive activity of a few boys. Very significant play can go on here, since blocks remain among the materials uniquely suited to the uses of many children, to work out and represent their ideas and understandings. This will only be realized if the teacher sees the value of blocks and works with the block builders actively to solve their problems, to add needed ideas or details, and to help them verbalize the understandings and relationships they have achieved. Sometimes, the block builders can discuss their problems or achievements with the whole class, to obtain ideas from other children, or to exchange suggestions for further progress. In this way, children can be led to raise their own aspirations for block construction and to learn from each other, or from the teacher, some solutions to problems of construction or perception or conception which may be of interest to them.

Motivating Dramatic Play

Most teachers are aware of the many kinds of props and costumes which can be made available to the housekeeping area to continue high interest in dramatic play. An increasing number of teachers are conscious of the need to stock not only women's clothing but also men's, and today it is a rare housekeeping corner which is without men's ties and shirts, army caps and jackets, and the like. Kindergarten teachers are often creative in the kinds of props they seek for the housekeeping corner, to stimulate more imaginative housekeeping area dramatic play. What needs to be added to this play is content, ideas, and understandings.

There were many examples in the economics study of children's playing out dramatically some of the learnings they were acquiring.

After a number of experiences involving cash register tapes, for example, including playing with tapes and discussing and reading the prices paid immediately upon returning from a marketing expedition to a supermarket, some of the new learnings became incorporated in dramatic play, as shown by the following recording:

> Several weeks after the children's marketing expedition, when Dorothy was playing customer and she received a tape from the storekeeper, she scrutinized it searchingly, then remarked laughingly to the researcher, "Sometimes when I get home and read my tape I say, 'Oh dear! I've spent too much money'."

As it began to be understood that it is the customer who pays the storekeeper for food purchases, rather than the other way around, the dramatic store play reflected this in many ways, of which the following are some examples:

> On March 19, money transactions were becoming more realistic. On that day, Eddie and Steve were storekeepers. Eddie, all excited, was waving his hands about and trying to attract Steve's attention.
> "Steve! Steve! Pat came and took something and he didn't pay for it," Eddie complained.
> Steve ran after Pat, shouting, "You didn't pay for your food. Give it back!" Steve took the food cans out of Pat's hands.
> "Oh, you make me burn," Pat exploded.

> On April 13, when Steve and David were storekeepers, they told their customers the store was not open, while they swept it with a broom and neatly arranged the food cartons on shelves. Betsy sneaked behind the counter and helped herself to some milk cartons. David intercepted her, took them away from her, shouting furiously, "You didn't pay." Betsy then came around to the front of the counter and ordered milk. David started to hand her the milk cartons, then withdrew them.
> "Have you any money?" he demanded suspiciously.
> "No," said Betsy.
> "Well, go home and get some from your mother," he said.
> Betsy ran to the housekeeping corner, then ran back, telling David plaintively that she couldn't find any money. Thereupon David gave her some paper money.
> This incident indicated that David realized it is the customer who has to pay the storekeeper, but being a realist he shared his "money" with Betsy so that the play could proceed.

> Henry, Eddie, and Mona were storekeepers on April 26, and Steve was a customer.

"I want to buy something," Steve announced.

"Do you have any money?" asked Eddie.

"No, I don't," Steve replied.

"Then you can't buy anything," said Eddie, flatly.

Steve then went to the next-door housekeeping corner and he returned with Mona, each with fistfuls of paper money. They counted out their bills and made some purchases.

The teacher's active role in helping to introduce some beginnings of reality in price concepts was another example of adult introduction of ideas into the children's play. When children asked for help in writing price signs for the store, the teacher suggested realistic prices, such as twenty-five cents for a quart of milk and fifty-nine cents for one dozen eggs. When the teacher played the role of a customer and was charged forty dollars for a can of juice, she protested it was too expensive. When the student teacher played the role of a customer and was charged two cents for a quart of milk, she told the children she was getting a bargain, that the price was cheap.

Content was added to children's ideas for dramatic play when the teacher invited the supermarket manager to visit the class to discuss pricing, jobs and other information with the children. The discussion brought out, for example, that there are different kinds of milk and that skimmed milk is cheaper than whole milk. Other content discussed included such ideas as the store's need to make money in order to stay in business, by charging customers higher prices than the store paid to farmers for food; that the manager's job is to see that everyone else does his work; and that food purchases are made from farmers in large quantities by stores.

Toward the end of the study, on May 2, Pat was playing storekeeper and began to reflect some of these new ideas in his play as follows:

Pat was playing storekeeper, telephoning. He was ordering groceries. He asked for paper, he had a pencil, and he wrote some numbers on a paper while talking on the telephone. When he hung up, the researcher asked what he had written on his paper and he showed it to her, saying, "Eighty, and this looks like four thousand to me."

"It does to me, too," said the researcher. "What are the numbers?"

"How many things I have to get, how many eggs I have to get . . . ," Pat replied.

"Oh, you're ordering groceries for the store?"

"Yes," said Pat.

Many more examples could be cited of the ways in which children ordered and organized their thinking and clarified their understandings through dramatic play.

ORGANIZING
FOR LEARNING

Organizing follows planning. If the plan calls for a specific phonograph record, it must be available when needed, and there must be a phonograph in good working order. If new materials are going to be introduced, how are they to be introduced? Will children have to take turns, should self-selection be permitted, and, if it is, what choices will be available to the rest of the class? The murmur of disappointment so often heard in a kindergarten when some shiny new equipment is introduced which only two children may use on one day is avoidable, if the plan and the classroom organization provides for several equally attractive centers of interest at one time.

Instead of assuming that the same basic equipment will serve all purposes, teachers can add or remove equipment as needed. If new material is introduced, it is important to organize the manner, time, and place of introduction. The teacher can either allow the material to be discovered or introduce it with explanation, supervision, and guidance. The setting can be organized to allow the children to see some of the possibilities for the use of new materials.

The teacher provides information in many forms, including trips into the community, bringing community resources into the classroom, providing first-hand experiences in cooking, sewing, carpentry, or any other activity, as well as through movies, filmstrips, television, books, and pictures. "Telling" children is not usually the most effective way to offer five-year-olds usable information or ideas. Neither does play, by itself, insure concept development. Even when the play is structured and focused on some desired concepts, play must be integrated with other methods to contribute to concept learning. All this requires the teacher's organizing efforts.

Other organizing steps may consist of seeking authoritative information, practicing a song or story, preparing a map or chart or diagram, ordering supplies, evolving the details for some evaluative techniques or hanging pictures on the bulletin board.

The organizing activities of kindergarten teachers are more time-consuming than most school administrators realize. To encourage activities required for organizing for learning, school supervisors and administrators might acknowledge this necessary adjunct to teaching and plan to free the teacher during the day for a period adequate to accomplish needed and desirable chores. In many schools, the kindergarten teacher is the only one who is working with two different classes every day, without any time during the school day for accomplishing the many tasks that must be done. Other grade level teachers may have an occasional hour during the week when art, music, or physical education teachers work with their classes. But this is very rare for teachers of five-year-olds.

Teachers can never hope to leave the school behind them entirely when they go home, because some chores can only be done away from school, and productive thinking cannot be turned on or off at will. Understanding that this is so, school administrators may seek to limit teachers' burdens by making it possible for them to perform some of their necessary organizing activities at school on school time, when other school personnel are available for consultation, if needed.

Sometimes the teacher organizes the classroom for a directed discussion with all or part of the group. The teacher's organizing plans must include timing the discussion so that it can be initiated when children are not restless and have not been engaged in spectator activities just prior to a period when they will be asked to sit relatively quietly for a time. Creating an atmosphere conducive to cooperative and fruitful discussion is essential and important elements are physical room arrangements as well as stimulating and challenging materials to look at, listen to, describe, ask questions about, or refer to. The routines by which children assemble for a discussion can be orderly, well-understood, and efficient or disorderly and so disorganized as to delay discussions, waste time, and contribute to children's feelings of impatience and restlessness. When the teacher plans discussions with a small group, she must also plan the work of the rest of the class, if her discussion is not to be interrupted.

Often, a very small change or novelty makes a disproportionately large contribution to fresh stimulation and thinking. For example, boys bored with block structures can be offered some pulleys, wire, switches, springs, hooks, a flashlight or other simple hardware, to challenge some new and purposeful, imaginative play. Block construction and dramatic play often take new directions after a stimulating trip. Small props made by children at the carpentry table are helpful accessories to play. Children do not usually develop the meanings and relationships inherent in new ideas by themselves. The teacher's role in extending and clarifying ideas cannot be overemphasized.

GROUPING
FOR LEARNING

Some teachers are very skillful in grouping the children for learning activities so that much is accomplished. This is not just a matter of separating two personalities which appear to be combustible in combination. The grouping discussed here involves the teacher's understanding of how young children learn and her arranging, placing, and working with them in groups which are of optimum size for the purpose at hand.

For some purposes, the group should only consist of one child at a time either because of the nature of the content or the needs of the child. Sometimes, the teacher can work with groupings of two or three children, or seven or eight, depending upon what is to be accomplished and which children and how many can be expected to work together for any length of time. A movie, filmstrip, or visitor may indicate a total-group learning experience, but there may be special considerations which suggest excusing one or two children for other work.

Optimum grouping in the classroom is accomplished through experimentation and a tentative approach. The only imperative to good grouping is the teacher's understanding of the experimental nature of her efforts. In time, for any group of children, the teacher begins to abstract some guiding principles which lend more security to the decisions she makes. Where the discipline problems overshadow the learning opportunities, the teacher is safe in concluding that some other grouping might turn out to be more successful.

There is always the chance that it is not the grouping but the content which requires changing.

Too often, teachers abandon excellent plans for intellectual content because of the poor reception the children accord the initial steps. Sometimes this is merely a matter of changing from a total-class discussion to one which involves no more than six or eight children. Suddenly, when the teacher makes this change, experiences become satisfying intellectual challenges which had previously been frustratingly negative.

Grouping practices will not, by themselves, remedy shortcomings in the nature of the experiences planned for children. Abstract, didactic teaching is usually no more successful with one child than with twenty-five. However, if the teacher plans an intensive discussion in which she proposes to be aware of individual responses and contributions, she is bound to be more effective in accomplishing her objective with a smaller rather than a larger group. On the other hand, if she wishes to stimulate considerable interchange and exchange of information, the larger group may be better able to accomplish this purpose.

Meeting Needs of Individual Children

It may be that the single, most crucial, test of the appropriateness of any kindergarten curriculum is the extent to which it meets the needs of the individual children in the class. In order to meet the needs of real children, a program cannot be one which is completely prepackaged and preplanned. The teacher must understand how flexibly content can be manipulated to satisfy and challenge different children as they reveal their individuality and unique problems each year.

Some school systems have experimented for years with alternative methods of grouping children for instruction to maximize individualized teaching. Grouping is only an arrangement for teaching which is based on beliefs about the way differently grouped children respond to instruction. It must be somehow accomplished in every school. Grouping undoubtedly affects the teacher's ability to instruct and educate children, as well as the ability of the children in the class to use the instruction offered to them. Unfortunately, there is little scientific evidence of the precise nature of the interaction of these factors.

There is apparently no grouping panacea by which to bypass the teacher's important job of learning to know, understand, and teach the children in her class. Ordinarily, the teacher looks for the usual wide range of abilities, interests, experiences and needs, knowing how much difference will appear even in a small class of five-year-olds.

How is the teacher to determine how well her curriculum is meeting the needs of the children in her class? If she has good evaluative procedures, she will be collecting and analyzing the kind of information and evidence which will throw much light on this essential question. But while she is collecting and storing this information, she can also become aware of some of the factors she can gauge from day to day. Meeting the needs of individual children requires a knowledge of their strengths, problems, and personality variations. The teacher can arrange the program to provide opportunities to become better acquainted with the children, to observe them alone or in interaction with each other, to spend a few minutes daily with each child either in responding to his requests or on her own initiative.

The teacher, then, assesses the kindergarten curriculum for the kinds of opportunities it offers her to know and work with children as individuals, and for the opportunities it offers children to work with content and materials which are meaningful for them. The curriculum suggestions made in this book, and the teaching techniques suggested, are geared to meeting the needs of individual children and to maximizing the individualization of instruction. One requirement of this approach is the condition that the content have intellectual challenge for the children in the class and that this content be made available in such a way as to have meaning for such children. This seems essential to any program which is educative for children of any age.

Organizing Practice Activities

Children often make discoveries and fail to realize what they have discovered or what possible relationships such discoveries may have to anything else. Their lack of experience in naming, categorizing, and generalizing frequently contributes to their losing sight of a discovery soon after it is made or remembering it vaguely or in some distorted form. Unstable concepts are subject to such vagaries and teachers must be aware that children develop concepts gradually and require practice opportunities to help them materialize, concretize, and verbalize new ideas before they can become stable and dependable. Children need practice under varying conditions before the real meanings of the concept become clear, in order to achieve either differentiation from other concepts or generalization, or both.

In the study of economic concepts, some specific cases of practice opportunities can be cited. For example, one concept which was studied in several different ways was the place of machinery in modern economic production and some of the advantages of machine technology. The children studied machines by using some small ones in the classroom, such as hammers, a movie projector, and an ice cream freezer, noting and observing machines used in food stores, studying and discussing pictures of different kinds of machines used in food production and distribution, seeing a movie about machines and in many other ways. A practice activity followed the second showing of the movie, "How Machines and Tools Help Us," [9] in the form of a class discussion in which the teacher guided the children to sort out their observations, to make generalizations, clarify their conceptions, to help the children stabilize their emerging concepts. Children were guided to formulate and express ideas they already had and then to go on from there to perceive some of the significance they had not previously noticed.

Another practice activity, requiring the children to report to the class the next day on the kinds of machines used in their own homes, sharpened some dimensions of the category "machine" which had not been obvious before. One child described television as "something you see that's not in your house but it could be far away in another country." Another child pointed out that we see things in newspapers too, and another said we can hear things on radio. One child generalized the difference, saying, "Only on television you see them move."

Thus in studying machines there were practice activities to recall

[9] "How Machines and Tools Help Us," Chicago: Coronet Films.

learnings, to distinguish between items as well as to find some of the attributes which unite separate objects into a category. This helped children to find out what they knew, to recall and use the language needed to express it, so that it could be thought about and discussed. It also helped children to store information in a form in which it seemed more likely to remain accessible and recognizable, and to use the growing store of information to begin to provide the shape of a meaningful generalization.

Practice opportunities need not be verbal. In fact, many practice situations in most kindergartens tend to be of the nonverbal variety, such as opportunities children have to organize and express their ideas in clay, paint, crayon, blocks, and other such unstructured media. It is the verbal opportunities which tend to be infrequent and have therefore been stressed here. It should be noted that these verbal opportunities were planned after children had had many other active experiences and expressive opportunities. It should also be noted that the practicing concerned labels, categories, and concepts, after children had had substantial experiences from which the nature of the concepts could have been discovered or perceived.

Repetition under varying conditions should be featured in order to develop concept stability. If "producers" are being studied, children can be guided to extract and differentiate such concepts in real-life situations (such as, who are the "producers" one sees in a supermarket or on a street), from pictures and games, in role-playing in dramatic play, and in movies and filmstrips, as well as in remote and unfamiliar contexts. A concept which can be carried intact, recognized, and differentiated in a variety of situations and contexts is one which can be regarded as stable and well-understood. Perhaps most five-year-olds will fail to show such stability. Perhaps they may only achieve semi-stability and instability in relation to any concept of complexity and significance. It can be expected that most kindergarten children will rarely develop concepts beyond the beginning stage. But this is the most difficult of all stages, the initial perception and cognition of first meanings. This is the necessary base for further learnings, new experiences and more complex organization of the understandings learned. If the results may appear to be very small, they must be valued as the base without which significant meanings cannot be learned.

CLARIFYING IDEAS

Children can carry erroneous ideas with them for long periods before opportunities occur for clarification. This can happen when there are too few opportunities for children to express their ideas or for the teacher to become aware of them.

Children are assumed to learn from first-hand experiences. When children play out their understandings, it must be assumed that they are exchanging erroneous ideas and misconceptions, along with valid conceptions. It is essential that young children's learning by doing be supplemented by teaching methods designed to uncover and clarify their ideas. As Wann has stated,

> Children collect information from many sources. Much of the information with which they are confronted is disorganized and can be miseducative as well as educative. Children need help in thinking about this information. They need help in putting these ideas into proper relationships. They need help in their quest to know and to learn.[10]

Clarifying children's ideas does not always call for a one-to-one relationship. If the daily plan of work includes a substantial period of time when children may pursue self-selected interests, the teacher has time to move about the room, making suggestions and offering her services where needed. She also listens and records some brief notes, or checks a list which includes various items she wishes to record for evaluation or diagnosis of learnings. In order to use the children's work period in this way, the teacher must be free from other chores at this time. Kindergarten teachers need help with their burdensome record-keeping, either through the provision of teacher assistants or through automation.

Besides freeing the teacher from nonteaching chores, it is also necessary to teach the children to work independently. Some classes can become highly organized for such work rapidly while other groups may require more time to develop the needed self-discipline.

Children indicate and express their ideas in innumerable ways. Their art work is helpful in showing the teacher their attitudes,

[10] Kenneth D. Wann et al., *Fostering Intellectual Development in Young Children*, New York: Teachers College Press, Teachers College, Columbia University, 1962, p. 118.

values, hopes, and needs, as well as the content of their ideas. Children's responses to music and dance are other sources of information. Their contributions to sharing activities, to group discussions, their comments or questions about stories and books, are all informative. So are the roles they play in dramatic play, the carpentry projects they undertake, and the block constructions they build. Naturally the most important way children express ideas is verbally. The teacher also uses verbal methods in helping children clarify their ideas. Some of these verbal methods include questions, comments, corrections, definitions, and instructions.

It is surprising to note the range of concepts with which young children attempt to deal. Wann's study found three-, four-, and five-year-olds trying to deal with a wide range of concepts, including such basic ones as death, time, God, and weather.[11] Television and other mass media introduce young children to some of the most significant and abstract themes of our culture. Attempts can be made to discover what children understand of this bombardment of information. Clearly, the impact is different on different children, varying with socio-economic factors, emotional and maturational characteristics, and supporting and interacting cultural factors.[12]

Some kindergarten teachers might object that if they must find ways to clarify children's ideas it could only be accomplished at the expense of a kindly, unpressured atmosphere. Children are not harmed by efforts to help them to understand new vocabulary and ideas unless there are elements of compulsion, hostility, invidious comparisons, punishment or disapproval for lack of achievement, and elimination of needed play and work periods. These elements would be undesirable for children at any age. No one would advocate them for five-year-olds.

THE TEACHER'S ROLE
AS A RESOURCE PERSON

How much expertise can any one teacher be expected to have? The numerous and varied demands on kindergarten teachers suggest

[11] *Ibid., passim.*
[12] Wilbur Schram, *Television and the Lives of Our Children*, Stanford, Calif.: Stanford University Press, 1961.

that, if some depth and competence can be attained in at least one area, teachers can develop some interests and hobbies upon which to build further competence. Strong supervisory and administrative support could promote sharing of teachers' varied talents for the benefit of the maximum number of children.

Sometimes a better music program results if two classes combine to work with the teacher who is especially skillful at the piano or whose voice and musicality are stimulating to the children. Additional specialists are sometimes needed to supplement the teachers' resources.

The teacher can become a resource person in a number of fields in which she is not expert, if she reads widely, pursues some creative hobbies, and desires further personal and professional growth. Sometimes a teacher becomes a resource person by accident. She might be the only teacher in a school who was brought up on a farm and has personal acquaintance, memories, stories, relatives, and perhaps some realia of farm life. Other teachers may become resource persons because of the trips they have made, the collections they have assembled, the ownership of some unusual object (as a spinning wheel or a butter churn), or some unusual ability such as good chess playing. Some teachers turn out to be invaluable resource persons simply because of the splendid human qualities they have of compassion, optimism, wisdom, and warm friendliness.

Teachers can also be helped to develop additional resources. Schools which own musical instruments can make these available to teachers as well as to students for lessons and practice. In one school, an assistant principal taught a group of teachers to play guitar, meeting once a week on the lunch hour. Appreciation, encouragement, and recognition of growth in interest and skills are likely to net the school happier and more inspired teachers.

All teachers can develop resource files which can be shared within a school, including pictures, songs, annotated lists of records, books and collections of objects. Teachers now return from trips with collections of sea shells, colorful beach pebbles, acorns and pine cones, puff balls and "polly noses," fungi, mosses and ferns, assorted rocks, pictures, slides, and movies. Resources of individual teachers can be increased by more "kits" for specific purposes, preplanned and preassembled for their use. Schools can pool resources and share expensive or difficult-to-assemble combinations of items and materials. Staff planning and evaluation of these "kits" and designs for new ones would assure investment of school funds in materials most likely to be valued, understood, and used by classroom teachers. Such kits are becoming increasingly available in the area of science and could be fruitful in other areas as well.

THE TEACHER'S ROLE AS A SCHOLAR

Busy teachers are expected to know more today in order to guide young children to find answers to questions and learn to love the pursuit of knowledge. Teachers can look to many sources to try to keep up with the flood of new ideas.

Radio and television newscasts as well as a good daily newspaper are sources used by most teachers for the latest news. Professional organization meetings and journals are indispensable for teachers, for awareness of current thinking and trends. Courses at colleges and universities are needed to keep up with one's field. Teachers' reading and recreational interests inevitably benefit their students in one situation or another.

Teachers may cooperate to build substantial school libraries to serve their needs as well as the needs of children. Teachers need easy access to professional journals, research studies, encyclopedias, and special information sources. Teachers may clarify their own ideas in discussion groups to share professional interests, concerns, or new ideas. Such meetings may feature reports of visits to other schools, interesting educational experiences, or demonstrations of new materials and methods. In some cases, teachers may request professional organizations to plan meetings in which new research is featured.

DECISION-MAKING

It can be argued that the teacher today does not make important curriculum decisions but instead carries out the decisions and detailed instructions of teachers' manuals and guides. It can also be argued that, no matter how detailed are the instructions which the teacher is following, once she closes her door in her self-contained classroom, her class will experience a uniquely different lesson from the one experienced by any other class. The burden of evidence today favors the view that the teacher makes important curriculum decisions.

Jones points out that while curriculum innovations can originate from a variety of sources, "it is the teacher who controls the curriculum." [13] The teacher is the one who can make innovations effective because of her own convictions and excitement or she can guarantee that new practices will fail.

It is the teacher in the final analysis who decides the kind of program children experience regardless of the nature of the syllabus provided for the kindergarten. The teacher who believes that limited objectives of social and emotional growth plus some simple facts about seasons, weather, and holidays are sufficient will delimit the curriculum to experiences which will accomplish these objectives. The teacher who recognizes that five-year-olds today are challenged to find out about their world will provide experiences that help to answer their questions and encourage them to think about their world.

Researchers continue to find that children are able to cope with much more content and ideas than they have been accustomed to. Cammarota, who studied the introduction of a new social studies program in the primary grades of Bucks County, Pennsylvania, schools, concluded that primary children today should work with "difficult" as well as "easy" ideas, that children are interested in people and places far away and not only enjoy map work but have little difficulty understanding it.[14] Yet it is easy to misinterpret findings such as these, to mean that all children learn best from books and workbooks and that there is no difference in the way that younger children learn. Such conclusions are *not* implicit in such findings, as most teachers of young children can readily attest.

Unfortunately, many kindergarten teachers are finding various impositions thrust upon them by well-meaning supervisors and administrators who desire to reassure the community that their school aims at the rigor and excellence which everyone nowadays is supposed

[13] Lloid B. Jones, "Curriculum Innovations in a Public School System," *Theory and Practice*, 1962 (Oct.), 1:201.

[14] Gloria Cammarota, "New Emphases in Social Studies for the Primary Grades," *Social Education*, 1963, 27(2):78–79.

to accomplish. These frequently take the form of highly formalized reading-readiness or reading programs or a formal, workbook-centered arithmetic program. Many such programs specify methods of teaching which are unsuitable for young children's ways of learning.

Kindergarten teachers who are thoughtful and scholarly will make curriculum decisions which will open many facets of man's knowledge to children's beginning exploration and discovery. They need considerable freedom of choice as to *how* to accomplish desirable learnings and skills in ways appropriate to five-year-olds. They need more guidance and opportunity to contribute to decisions as to what the objectives should be and how these can be translated into the working behavioral terms which begin to suggest promising activities and experiences.

GUIDING THE LEARNING PROCESS

The young child's need to establish a good relationship with an adult in order to be able to learn is exceedingly well-documented in the literature of early childhood education, which it is not the function of this book to expand.

However, it is often assumed that teachers must choose between fostering children's intellectual development and establishing good relationships with children. This is a false set of alternatives. There can be no worthwhile program for children without excellent child-teacher relationships. Why, then, should teachers assume they must sacrifice good relationships if they are to achieve intellectual progress?

The either-or position rests on one or more implicit assumptions. One is that teachers would have to ignore individual differences and require the same degree of intellectual progress of all children, which would create considerable tension and difficulty. Another possible assumption is that only by strict disciplinary procedure could intellectual progress be achieved because young children are not otherwise likely to become interested and involved in programs geared to develop ideas and concepts. Or there could be the assumption that intellectual progress is achieved only through books, requiring all young children to learn to read. As these assumptions are stated, it becomes apparent that none of them are valid.

Perhaps a reluctant teacher really objects to the role proposed for her here because she has not experienced it and because it is different from the usual conception of the kindergarten teacher's role. The image of the nondirective teacher has long been the standard in kindergarten practice. This type of teaching is one of "knowing" the child, through intensive child study, setting the stage, and carefully refraining from active intervention in the child's activities in school, except to enforce discipline. Such a concept of the teacher's role has grown from the psychological and psychiatric orientation of much of the current literature on teaching young children.

The teacher's role is different from that of the therapist or analyst. The latter are concerned to establish relationships which will make possible emotional therapy for which teachers are not qualified. Teachers are educated to guide children's learning experiences, which require quite a different kind of relationship. Teaching frequently requires very active intervention into the learning process, in order to move it forward.

Without assistance from the teacher, the child has to struggle through trial-and-error learning which becomes increasingly inefficient and frustrating. The nondirective teacher offers warmth and approval where the child's real need may be a road map or some hints to help him make an intuitive leap or recognize what he needs to look for. While each child must do his own learning, he needs the knowledgeable kind of teacher guidance which not only spurs him on to search, but provides some needed tools and experiences which can move him forward with satisfaction along the learning continuum. The directive teacher can supply needed tools and materials because she has a plan toward which she is working and because this plan is consonant with the young child's learning needs.

The directive teacher seeks to make some contribution to the learning process, with questions, materials, suggestions, and experiences that help the child make progress toward clearly stated goals. She assumes children cannot be creative out of ignorance. Everything they experience sparks their interest and curiosity and spurs their desire for exploration and manipulation. The teacher creates an exciting learning environment within the classroom, in order to stimulate more meaningful, learning-oriented activities. The directive teacher does not assume that the child understands the ideas and relationships which exist within the phenomena he perceives. Instead, she finds ways to make these explicit in active learning experiences and to stabilize them in practice situations. She is highly selective in the content she offers because she has some specific learning outcomes in mind.

Directive teaching points to the need for occasional novelty and dramatic content to maintain interest over long enough periods for children to begin to make discoveries. The dynamics of interpersonal relationships are essential tools of the directive teacher as she guides the individual child in his learning.

It is important to note that directive teaching does more than help children advance their intellectual learnings. Children who are challenged to explore their environment and who are supplied with appropriate tools and direction for their exploration are likely to make considerable progress in their emotional and social growth. Teachers who choose to try out some of the approaches outlined in this book will find that their relationships with children and the classroom atmosphere will improve.

Some progress in classroom relationships will occur with the decline of discipline problems due to boredom. Eagerness for learning is enhanced by an intellectually stimulating environment where children are involved in manipulative, exploring activities of interest to them. In addition, when there is appropriate intellectual challenge, it is possible to organize the classroom for children's independent work, freeing the teacher for the kind of individual work with each child which is warm, personal, and knowledgeable and which can grow into understanding, sympathy, and realistic appreciation.

Offering children intellectual stimulation and expecting achievement and growth from them should enhance the self-image of the child, help strengthen weak egos, and establish a sense of personal worth and dignity. Children's growing sense of mastery and ability to cope with some of the important ideas and issues of contemporary life should contribute to growth of independence, responsibility and love of learning.

The expectation that parents and school personnel will respond positively to the kind of program which has specific learning goals, even though these are not book-oriented, should contribute to greater esteem of kindergarten education. In the face of the great pressure of contemporary society upon young children to achieve today, it would benefit the five-year-old to see reflections from adults in the community that his kindergarten learning is worthwhile and meaningful.

The active approach the teacher must take to help children develop concepts has been termed here directive teaching. This requires active intervention and assistance in the child's learning as well as planning for specific behavioral goals. Teaching of this kind, it has been suggested, is favorable to the development of good teacher-child relationships and to the pursuit of mental health.

BIBLIOGRAPHY

Almy, Millie, *Ways of Studying Children*, New York: Teachers College Press, Teachers College, Columbia University, 1959.

Blough, Glenn O., and Marjorie H. Campbell, *Making and Using Classroom Science Materials in the Elementary School*, New York: Holt, Rinehart and Winston, 1954.

Bruner, Jerome S., *On Knowing*, Cambridge, Mass.: Belknap Press of Harvard University Press, 1962.

———, "Needed: A Theory of Instruction," *Educational Leadership*, 1963, 20:523–532.

Cammarota, Gloria, "New Emphases in Social Studies for the Primary Grades," *Social Education*, 1963, 27(2):77–80.

Dinkmeyer, Don, and Rudolf Dreikurs, *Encouraging Children to Learn: The Encouragement Process*, Englewood Cliffs, N.J.: Prentice-Hall, 1963.

Hammond, Sarah Lou, Ruth J. Dales, Dora Sikes Skipper, and Ralph L. Witherspoon, *Good Schools for Young Children*, New York: Macmillan, 1963.

Jefferson, Blanche, *Teaching Art to Children*, Boston: Allyn and Bacon, 1959.

Jones, Lloid B., "Curriculum Innovations in a Public-School System," *Theory and Practice*, 1962 (Oct.), 1:197–201.

McClelland, David C., and Others, *The Achievement Motive*, New York: Appleton-Century-Crofts, 1953.

Milner, Ernest J., *You and Your Student Teacher*, New York: Teachers College Press, Teachers College, Columbia University, 1954.

Peterson, Dorothy G., "The Teacher's Professional Reading," *Elementary School Journal*, 63, October 1962, pp. 1–5.

———, *The Elementary School Teacher*, New York: Appleton-Century-Crofts, 1964.

Schramm, Wilbur, *Television and the Lives of Our Children*, Stanford, Calif.: Stanford University Press, 1961.

Taba, Hilda (Director), *Thinking in Elementary School Children*, San Francisco: San Francisco State College, 1964.

Wann, Kenneth D., Miriam Selchen Dorn, and Elizabeth Ann Liddle, *Fostering Intellectual Development in Young Children*, New York: Teachers College Press, Teachers College, Columbia University, 1962.

7

EXPERIENCES
AND MATERIALS

In the organization of programs for intellectual competence in the kindergarten it becomes apparent that there is no single type of experience or single kind of educational material or equipment that will serve all of the needs of thinking children. The intellectual growth of children is dependent upon the integrated, planned, purposeful use of a variety of experiences and activities organized to develop specific concepts. Although the availability of certain kinds of materials in the classroom is a necessary part of a program for intellectual development, neither the existence of certain pieces of equipment in the room, nor the development of specific kinds of experiences will guarantee maximum intellectual growth in the children. This can only be accomplished by the teacher's synthesis of a variety of experiences and the use of many kinds of materials concentrating on specific learning.

Materials, equipment, and experiences are in reality the tools and the raw materials of education. By themselves they are as artless as a block of marble and a set of chisels. But given to the right teacher they will blossom forth into exciting and significant educational experiences that will move children ahead in their development. The teacher must understand the potentials and limitations of each experience she offers to her class so that as the year progresses, the total kindergarten experience emerges as a meaningful, significant, integrated whole.

DEVELOPING
MEANINGFUL
EXPERIENCES

Experiences aimed at fostering intellectual development include those which present new information to children as well as those experiences which enable children to transform their information into meaningful conceptualizations. This includes experiences which allow children to investigate, collect, test, practice, integrate, and organize ideas. Additional experiences are those which permit children to communicate or express their developing ideas, and to develop language necessary to deal with ideas. These latter experiences are dealt with separately in Chapter 8, in order to stress their importance.

In order to present new information to children, a variety of in-class experiences can be developed in the kindergarten. These include realistic experiences and the presentation of information through books, stories, films, filmstrips, television shows, discussions, pictures, and artifacts. Many types of community resources can be brought into the classroom to supplement these experiences. In addition, children can be taken on field trips to various places in the community.

Field Trips

No classroom can possibly offer all of the potential learning activities that children might be able to use. The limitations of space and money require that the materials and equipment in any classroom must be highly selective. Children often have to be offered models or representations of real things instead of real objects. For these and other reasons, trips play a vital role in the kindergarten program. Trips extend the child's knowledge of his environment. They give him a chance to test his concepts against reality. They enable the child to experience real life situations that could never be duplicated within the four walls of the classroom.

The kindergarten child is limited in his experiences and understandings. He does not have the skill or background to use the many secondary sources of information. He still cannot decode the symbols of the written language. Even the symbols of communication that are understood by him—pictures and the spoken word—have limited meaning for him if he does not have in his background the experiences to supply the referents that give meaning to these symbols. For example, a three-year-old who knew airplanes only as small toys she could hold in her hand was puzzled to learn that her playmate's entire family had gone to California by plane. Her misconception of an airplane's size grew out of her lack of experience with the real object.

Field trips can be invaluable in helping the child to gather and assimilate knowledge and develop more complete understandings about the real world. On a field trip the child can bring all of his senses to bear on the problem of gathering information. He can see an object in its natural environment. He can get an undistorted picture of size, shape, depth, texture, color, and movement that are somehow lost when an object is experienced in some secondary manner. One does not know a community, for example, until one has experienced it with all of its characteristic sounds, sights, and smells.

There is also an emotional impact in taking a trip that adds to the learning experience. The excitement of planning and anticipating what will happen, the experience of being on a bus, of going past new and different places, enhances the child's learning. One young child, for example, who had recently flown extensively in South America with his parents was thrilled when his class took a short train ride from Milwaukee to the nearby station of Racine. This boy, who had traveled thousands of miles in his short life, had never been on a train. The short ride and the stop for lunch added a strong emotional impact to the total learning experience. It made the learning experience more memorable and more "rememberable" to the child. These feelings could never have been developed with travel posters or motion pictures of trains in action.

Trips can serve a multiplicity of purposes. The purpose of the trip will determine its organization and structure as well as its planning. Trips should have a particular aim in view. A trip may be planned to help children become acquainted with a particular place or area.

Such a trip may be a walk through the school building or around the block or school neighborhood. The teacher and children might stop at any interesting spot to investigate or explore further. Often, children will come up with some interesting learnings about a neighborhood that would astound even those most familiar with the area.

Exploratory trips often result in learnings about the community that feed into many areas of the curriculum including science, social science, and mathematics. Excavations and street repairs can sometimes be seen on such trips, especially in early spring when many potholes are being filled. Children can observe the effects of technology, the use of pneumatic drills, the melting of the asphalt, and the use of various tools. Questions can be raised about the tools, the processes and the role of the workers. Sometimes store windows offer a study in natural science. A group of children passing a fish store can be fascinated by the view of live lobsters slithering along on a bed of shaved ice. Studies in natural science can be furthered by finding out about the kinds of plants and trees there are in the neighborhood. "How many different kinds of flora can we find in the cracks in the sidewalks?" "How did the plants get into the vacant lots which no one has seeded?" "Why do we need traffic signs?" A multitide of such questions can be aroused by exploratory trips. Some of these questions will be deliberately overlooked by the teacher. Some can be used to stimulate interest in new areas of learning. Others can be used to illustrate those concepts the children have learned and mastered as they appeared in new context. The quality of children's questions tends to improve as their information and understanding increase.

More often a trip is selected to provide children with new information about a particular subject. The trip may be to a place that the children have not previously visited, although trips to familiar places are just as important. A child may visit the supermarket week after week as he accompanies his parents on shopping trips. The trip to the supermarket with the class becomes a wholly new experience, not because the place is unfamiliar, but because he now enters it with a different frame of reference and sees different things.

The questions a teacher may ask of the children can structure the experience so that the supermarket is as new to them as a visit to a strange city. Questions such as, "What kinds of workers do we have in the supermarket?" will enlarge the child's concept of supermarket from the simple one of a place to get food to the broader one of a place where services are produced, as well as received.

Trips can often give children information that cannot be gathered any other way. It is difficult, for example, to deal with concepts of the long-ago with children. A visit to a museum is valuable for seeing dioramas and artifacts representing things familiar to the children as they existed in the past. The understandings derived from such a trip can seldom be achieved in any other way.

Sometimes trips are used to correct specific misunderstandings or to help children develop specific concepts. Certain map concepts were difficult for the children to attain in the previously reported geography–history program. The children understood the definition of a map (a picture of a place) and its purposes (it tells you where to go), but experiences were necessary to develop the concepts of distance and direction and the idea of perspective. The map of the neighborhood and the trips taken through the neighborhood utilizing the map, described in Chapter 2, helped the children understand the concepts of "uptown," "downtown," and "crosstown," as represented on paper, and "north," "south," "east," and "west." The trip to the top of the tall building assisted in their forming several important concepts (given in detail in Chapter 2).

Taking more than one trip to the same place adds to the values that can come from a single trip. A trip to a botanical garden, for example, can provide much information about plants and shrubs and trees. The children can learn about the leaves of trees. They can compare the different flowers they see. By returning again to the same park, to the same trees and the same flowers the children can learn much more. They can go beyond their original categorizations of trees and their leaves as they watch the annual process by which some trees bud, grow leaves, change color, and become barren once more. They can compare these trees to those which remain green all year round, and learn that there are many ways in which trees differ from one another. They can become aware of the process of change in nature. The concept of seasons will take on new meaning as this process is understood. They can see animals behaving one way in summer and yet another in fall. The children can develop deeper concepts of the interrelationships of nature through these repetitive trips. The construction of a building over a period of time presents vivid pictures of change.

There are times, however, when it is valuable to take children to revisit a place, not because it will be different, but because the children's interim learnings permit them to view it in a different light. Teachers are often preoccupied with the need to "cover" a certain amount of work. They feel that trips should be made to as many diverse places as possible, and, of course, repeating a trip means the elimination of other trip possibilities. However, just as it can be valuable for a child to revisit ideas, it can be equally valuable for him to duplicate experiences to gain more mature insights.

Planning for trips is not the easiest part of teaching. Whenever the children are taken from the confines of their schoolroom their behavior tends to be less predictable. Often the highlight of a trip is overshadowed by some less important aspect, making some teachers feel that the trip was worthless. The teacher who took her children to observe ducks in the lake in a city park might have given up trips after this experience had she not understood the children. These children, who had discussed proper behavior before the trip, got off the bus and, instead of walking over to the duck pond, ran the entire length of a large meadow that was adjacent to it. The children came from overcrowded homes in an urban neighborhood where space was at a premium. The temptation to run in this large open space was irresistible. The teacher, realizing this, allowed the running while limiting its area. She legitimized the children's activity and modified her own goals for the trip.

Problems of behavior on trips can often be avoided with adequate planning. The teacher can anticipate most of the trouble spots if she is acquainted with the place to be visited. She will also attempt to include parents or other adults in the trip so that the burden is not hers alone. She will orient the other adults and the children to the trip, its organization and schedule, and the expected behavior of children. She will also carefully note what the children will see. Although there may only be a single opportunity to visit a museum, for instance, the teacher will select one or two exhibits that are appropriate for the topics being studied, thereby minimizing fatigue and mental indigestion.

Although trips are a significant element in the school program, it is seldom feasible for classes to take more than a few trips each year. Trips off school grounds create a liability problem. Some classes cannot take trips because the cost of transportation, which must be paid by the children, is prohibitive.

It seems evident, however, that if field trips are considered an important part of the school program they should be funded in the same way as films or filmstrips. Children are not expected to bring in nickels and dimes to cover film rental fees. However, if the cost of transportation for school trips must, in some school districts, continue to be paid out of funds the children contribute, steps ought to be taken to see that lack of funds does not prevent worthwhile excursions. Parent associations, local business people, and civic groups can be asked to contribute funds to insure that the teacher is not unduly limited by money problems. It would also be helpful if teachers developed a list of resources within walking distance. In many schools, especially those in the central sections of large cities, the communities surrounding the schools offer more opportunities for excursions than many teachers realize. Small industries, commercial establishments, and other enterprises are often willing to have visitors when they know the purpose and value of the visits.

Some trips are used as a break from the routine of learning, a reward to be used in various ways (for ending a unit of study, for example) or as a fun activity (the annual spring outing). When trips are not incorporated into the program they may have little educational value. The value of well planned trips does not end when children return to the classroom. It continues as the children recall their experiences in new contexts. Preparation and follow-up is necessary if maximum value is to be gained from trips.

Some guidelines for utilizing trips in the classroom situation can be culled from the works of earlier kindergarten leaders. Pratt, for example, used trips into the neighborhood extensively in her program. The children often went walking through the streets to the docks, and to various other parts of the city. They would return to school and reconstruct their observations in block building. The trips and block building were important parts of a total social studies program.[1]

Mitchell also used trips in social studies programs. Geography was studied as a laboratory science and therefore children's trips into the neighborhood were field studies. They were used to gather information from which the children could develop hypotheses or generalizations from the social sciences.[2]

The facts and information gathered on a trip need to be integrated with classroom activities. Four ways of achieving this are listed below.

1. *Art work*. This is often overdone and sometimes quite hackneyed, especially when it emerges from the directive of teachers to children upon returning to class from a field trip, "Now everyone take a sheet of paper and draw a picture of what you have seen or what you liked best about the trip." Children in such situations may learn to dread trips because of the necessity to produce something immediately upon return. Sometimes children find it too difficult to make sense out of new experiences immediately. Sometimes ideas and impressions have to percolate for awhile before they are fully brewed and ready for expression. In one case, for example, after a walk to the Hudson River, where the children observed the *Queen Mary* docking, the children returned to class and, after a short discussion, resumed their normal activities. That day not a single picture of the river or the ocean liner was drawn or painted by any of the children. Several days later a series of paintings and drawings were made spontaneously by the children. For the next two weeks, such pictures continued to be produced. The pictures showed many of the details of the boat and the docking procedure observed. The children not only incorporated their observations of the actual event in their pictures but other ideas associated with boats that they had gleaned from other classroom activities.

As children develop impressions, they can be led to some form of expression. The problems that arise often come, not from the children's lack of desire to express themselves, but from their need to think about, digest, and develop some understandings and reactions.

[1] Carolyn Pratt, *Experimental Practices in City and Country School*, New York: E. P. Dutton, 1924.

[2] Lucy Sprague Mitchell, *Young Geographers*, New York: John Day, 1934.

When there is time, and when ideas can be revisited, there need be no pressure on the child for immediate expression. There is no need to worry about moving on to another unit. The child can still deal with the same ideas several weeks from now. If he paints the picture later it will still be in context.

2. *Conversation.* Often teachers take time after a trip to talk about the experience with the children. This has several advantages. It provides the child with an opportunity to put his impressions into words, thereby providing a language base for new ideas; it allows opportunity for correction of confusions and misunderstandings; and it gives the child an opportunity to share his experiences with others and to compare his impressions with those of the other children in his class.

In conversations and discussions the teacher should be careful not to impose her views or impressions on the children. Otherwise she will find the children telling her about those things that are important to her and not to them. Young children sense when there is true freedom of discussion as opposed to having only the forms present. For discussions to be meaningful the child must feel that his contributions are valued. This does not mean total acceptance of every comment or the avoidance of questions or contributions by the teacher. Guidance and questioning are inevitable components of a discussion, but the teacher tempers her participation with sensitivity and genuine interest in the contributions of the children.

3. *Play activities.* Trips often lead the children to develop new dramatic play activities or to find new directions for play. This is more likely to happen if teachers make available to the children the kinds of props that they need to move the play forward. The teacher can also stimulate the play through clarifying comments which evoke memories of experiences the children had on the trips.

4. *Language arts activities.* A multitude of dramatic and language activities can be evoked by a trip, as indicated in Chapter 8.

Bringing Community Resources into the Classroom

It would be inefficient to take a field trip for every experience for which the classroom lacks the material, equipment, or personnel.

In many instances it is easier to "bring" the community into the classroom than to take the classroom out to the community.

Some places which children cannot visit can be viewed through film, filmstrips, or television. Available for classroom use are many good films on a broad spectrum of subjects. Although these cannot replace the trip for the multiplicity of learnings possible in a single experience, they are valuable. Television offers the added ingredient of immediacy to the vicarious experience. Through the medium of television, children can partake in many community affairs from which they would otherwise be barred for ohe reason or another. The launching of a rocket, the installation of a new mayor, the docking of the first ocean-going vessel after the seasonal opening of the St. Lawrence Seaway are exciting experiences that are primarily available to children through television.

There are many other ways that outside resources can be brought into the classroom to children. Civil service workers, such as firemen and policemen, are often assigned to visit schools and talk about their jobs as well as about such topics as safety. A supermarket manager or a local merchant may be willing to share information with a kindergarten class. Parents with interesting occupations or hobbies make excellent resource people. A generally untapped source of information is often available in many of the older persons in the community. Their first-hand knowledge of the history of the community and the changes that have taken place in many aspects of community life make them valuable in any social science program.

Aside from human resources there are other community resources that can be used, which may be different in each community. Some local museums will make available models and displays dealing with various natural and social phenomena. In some cities, zoos will lend live animals to be cared for by the children for a short period of time, or to be displayed and discussed for a few hours. Local businesses and industries may be tapped for other resources. State and local libraries may offer books in much greater variety than the classroom or school library. In one classroom, for example, a teacher was able to borrow an incubator from a local egg distributor which she used for hatching chicken eggs. Another teacher invited her uncle, a retired railroad worker, to visit her class when the children were studying transportation.

It might be helpful for teachers to develop lists of resources—objects and people—that can be brought into the classroom, so that selections can be made as needed. If teachers in a school could pool their lists, a much larger and more varied inventory could be available.

Realistic Experiences

So far in this chapter the discussion has been confined to the availability of realistic experiences in the educational life of the kindergarten child. As the real world is made accessible to the child, he is in a better position to observe, perceive and structure it, to develop significant concepts about it. The child is brought into contact with reality, aspects of which he would not otherwise meet, or which would not have the same meaning for him. More kinds of realistic experiences can be provided for the children in the kindergarten. Experience with many real situations and real things is as important in the young child's education as are play situations. Only through experience with the real phenomena of life can children develop the kinds of perceptions that lead to significant concept realizations.

Maria Montessori realized the educational value of realistic experiences when she developed the materials for practical life experiences in the Montessori school. Toys are a necessary part of the child's early experience but so are real things. Each serves a different purpose and they are not interchangeable. The young child in the housekeeping area "cooking" on a play stove is undergoing role exploration. The young child working with a teacher at a hot plate making applesauce out of fresh apples is learning about cooking as a process, about food chemistry, about the effect of heat on certain substances—all vital information out of which the formal concepts of science will grow. Despite some superficial resemblances these are quite different experiences serving very different purposes.

In the realm of realistic experiences are many activities which can lead to productive learning. In the area of science, for example, the concept of science as a process of inquiry cannot be taught without involving the children in active manipulation. By bringing in various kinds of phenomena and stimulating the children to explore them—posing questions, thinking through ways of answering their questions, gathering evidence, and trying to draw some conclusions from the evidence, the children can begin to act as scientists. Numerous experiences using both biological and physical phenomena can be developed in the kindergarten, as indicated in Chapter 5.

Experiences in cooking, woodworking, and other areas can also help to bring knowledge of realistic pursuits to the children in the classroom. Teachers can involve children in the processes of making useful objects. In this way they become aware not only of the process but also of the consequences of the process as they complete and use the product, whether it be a soup they have cooked or a stool they have built.

Teachers can also help children to move from dramatic play activities into realistic experiences that help further their understanding. In the economics study, for example, the children went from playing store to having a cookie sale. In the dramatic play activity they could solidify their understanding of the roles of consumer and producer and their relationship. But some concepts, such as that of profit, could not be explored in this play. As the teacher developed a situation where the children bought raw materials, produced goods and sold them for a price they could begin to gather information to clarify some of the elements of the concept of profit. Many concepts can only take shape through realistic experiences. Play, however, is a most important avenue of learning in the kindergarten program.

PLAY

Play is an essential factor in the learning process of children almost from the moment of birth. In the infant's first contacts with the environment, as he goes from random to purposeful activities, he gains much knowledge and information about his environment through play. As the child matures and becomes a preschooler, his play activities change. Dramatic play becomes an increasingly important element in his learning activities. His manipulative play becomes modified as well, as he gradually establishes more purpose and control. At these and later stages the child's play continues to present unique learning opportunities.

It has been said by many kindergarten educators that play is the work of the young child and that the child uses play to discover the outside world. The children in the classroom do not play for the purpose of learning. They play for the joy of playing. Play is a self-satisfying activity to them. The little girl who is actively cooking in the doll corner is not aware that she is exploring the maternal family role. She is enjoying the sheer fun of doing and acting that comes of spontaneous play. For children, play must be fun. It is the role of the teacher to provide additional values in play. Fortunately for early childhood education these two sets of goals are not mutually exclusive. The same set of activities can achieve both goals. The fact that significant learnings can develop from play need not detract from the children's satisfaction.

There is a difference between dramatic play and manipulative play. Dramatic play primarily focuses on the element of role playing. By its very nature it is symbolic activity. The child uses the information he has about his environment, miniaturizes life situations and acts them out. Manipulative play is neuromuscular kinesthetic activity and is less symbolic. Both are learning mechanisms. Neither has all the elements necessary for conceptual learning.

Dramatic Play

Dramatic play activity helps the child to symbolize activities and information, and put them into a meaningful framework. The child's conceptions of the world are tried out on a small scale as he plays through various roles and situations. New ideas are tested and are associated with others. They are practiced and solidified until meaningfulness is arrived at. Dramatic play contributes in many ways to learning.

Dramatic play alone will not guarantee conceptual learning. This form of play is simply one important path of the total learning process. Its success and usefulness rests upon the existence of other conditions in the classroom.

The breadth and extent of the child's play activities is dependent upon his previous experience and the information he has gathered from the outside world. In general, the child cannot go beyond this information in developing play activities. He is bound by his own experience. In order to have productive dramatic play activities, a solid base of experiences must be offered to the children. The visits in the research projects described in Chapters 2 and 3 to the harbor and the supermarket led the children to productive play centering on boats and supermarkets. It is quite possible that boat and store play could have developed without these experiences, but it seems certain that the play would not have continued over so long a period and with so much conceptual content.

As the research studies developed, the changes in the children's dramatic play were notable. The additional uses of money and cash register slips showed children using their newly acquired information and integrating it into already existing understandings. The dramatic play activities in these projects went beyond social interaction and emotional release. They included specific intellectual content and purpose, although the children continued to have fun.

The important ways in which the teacher can support dramatic play is by:

1. making additional information available to the children when the need arises.
2. structuring the play informally through the use of questions and suggestions.
3. providing adequate props when they are needed.
4. allowing adequate time for the children to play through their ideas.
5. helping children verbalize their understandings.

Manipulative Play

The variety of devices that can be supplied to children for manipulation is virtually unlimited. The teacher's selection depends upon the learnings to be gained and the materials available. Puzzles of various kinds, lotto games, models of real phenomena, and table games can all be used to help children develop concepts of the physical and social world. Manipulative play can take the form of various locking devices on a miniature door, a puzzle map of the United States or other devices. The material of manipulative play can be either real or representational, depending upon what is to be studied. In science, however, one can often use real phenomena.

Manipulative play offers opportunities to develop new concepts as children become increasingly aware of the attributes of certain phenomena. The repetitive aspects of children's play has been noted by all observers. This repetition represents practice. As children learn new skills or understandings they repeat the same activities until they achieve mastery.

In certain fields, especially in the areas of the sciences and mathematics, educational materials are already available in packaged form for classroom use, as indicated in Chapter 5. However, the same strides have not been made in developing manipulative material for the social studies. In this area the equipment companies have chiefly developed materials for dramatic play. Block accessories and sham storefronts can be purchased, often complete with miniature food packages and cash registers. More manipulative materials for each of the social studies areas needs to be developed. Perhaps imaginative teachers and equipment manufacturers will need to pool their ideas in order to begin to fill this need.

Three dimensional maps and globes would give children a better understanding of geographic concepts. Model communities and cities, or community kits complete with the various components including buildings, utility poles, railroad tracks, and shopping centers would help children to represent the geography of their immediate environment. Kits containing artifacts or facsimiles of artifacts can help children to develop some historical understandings. Concepts of historical time could be symbolized in concrete ways. These and other kinds of materials and equipment could be used to help children achieve better understandings and more reliable concepts in all the social sciences.

SELECTION OF LEARNING TOOLS

Our highly developed technology offers teachers of young children a bewildering variety of learning tools today. It is becoming difficult to keep up with the speed of industrial inventiveness and to select the most promising devices from many expensive items. Teachers will need assistance from research-oriented educational staffs to find out what is new and useful from the outpourings of educational supply-houses.

More encouragement of small-scale experimental programs which "try out" new devices to assess their usefulness could be helpful if findings could be disseminated quickly among teachers. Medical journals publish practitioners' analyses of their insights and hypotheses based on the narrow limits of their own practices. Perhaps teachers' journals of this type can serve the same purpose, to compare and exchange views and to pursue possibilities suggested by other practitioners.

If teachers can state more specifically than in the past the learning goals of their programs, the selection and evaluation of learning tools could become more objective and logical.

MATERIALS
AND EQUIPMENT

If you were to visit kindergartens throughout the United States, you would find the same materials and equipment regardless of the geographic location of the school. There would be differences in the quality and quantity of materials and equipment but remarkably little difference in the kinds of materials and equipment used. The materials and equipment offered kindergarten children reflect the established aims of kindergarten education, which have changed little in the past half century, although some variation does exist. Many kindergarten activities were originated by Froebel. These include such activities as music, arts and crafts, finger plays, and the circle activities. Other activities and materials now in use originated in the reform kindergarten movement and include blocks, the equipment in the housekeeping area, and doll play. Some play materials go back even further. Water and sand, for example, must have been play materials for children from the beginnings of the human race.

Each piece of material and equipment used in kindergarten has an important place in children's education. Most of these have withstood the test of time. This equipment reflects the kind of program that has been valued as educative for the young child. It is suggested here that intellectual learnings should have a larger place in the kindergarten program and that the big ideas from the bodies of knowledge could become the focus of the kindergarten program. Therefore it is necessary to evaluate the equipment and activities for their potential in stimulating and encouraging intellectual learnings. If the desired learning cannot be achieved through the available materials and equipment then steps need to be taken to provide for such learning through additional supplies and equipment.

Blocks

Many of the materials now in use in the kindergarten were originally designed for maximum flexibility. Equipment was designed so that children could determine its use and so that it would impose as little structure as possible on the child's activity. This prescription offers some excellent opportunities for aiding the development of intellectual understandings when used as a part of a total program.

Blocks are a prime example of flexible equipment because they can be used in countless ways. Children can build anything with blocks, and the structures so built can relate to a limitless variety of activities. Blocks can aid children to develop social science and mathematical concepts of many kinds.

Whether the blocks become a tool for developing social science concepts in a particular class depends mainly upon the teacher, the planning she does, the accessories she makes available, and the program she develops. The blocks themselves are a neutral element for learning. Block building can lead to significant intellectual goals if the teacher continually contributes ideas and information to the program. She does this through trips, language experiences, books, films, filmstrips, and a host of other communicative experiences. She also does this through her guidance of the play situation. The props she offers, the suggestions she makes, the questions she raises as the children go through their block building, can help the children advance in their learning within a framework of freedom of action, opportunity for creative expression, and minimal structuring by the teacher. A few suggestions can go a long way in guiding play.

Expressive Media

Many of the other materials and equipment found in the kindergarten are excellent expressive devices that can contribute immeasurably to the intellectual content of the program. Paints, clay, and crayons are tools by which children express not only feelings, but ideas. If the expression of ideas is valued, most of the arts and crafts media can be made to serve this aim. The paintings and drawings that children make, as well as the comments that often accompany these productions, are guides to the integrative intellectual processes that are developing in the minds of youngsters. When children are offered opportunities to use expressive media, they are assisted in their attempts to integrate and structure their knowledge about the world. In the attempt to express ideas through the creative media, children have to organize and integrate their understandings. These understandings are shaped by the many ways the teacher helps children to gather and interpret information.

Using Audio-Visual Devices

Many audio-visual devices are already available to kindergarten teachers interested in developing significant concepts in the various disciplines. Often the available devices have not been fully exploited in terms of the potential impact on intellectual development. The production of fruitful materials is hampered by a lack of imagination on the part of those who produce, as well as some educators who use, these materials.

In general the technical aspects of audio-visual instructional aids are superior in quality to their content. This is especially true of devices and materials for young children. We have countless automatic and semi-automatic devices today so simple that any nursery school child can operate them. However, content that is both sufficiently elementary and significant is not necessarily available to go with them.

Most kindergarten children can operate phonographs. Tape recorders using tape cartridges are just as simple. Teachers can use these to offer additional audio material to the class, ranging from songs, stories and poems to other information that can be meaningful for children on an auditory level. When the class is studying animals, for example, recordings of animal calls can be played. Interviews with resource people can be recorded and played back to children as can the sounds of different languages. The content of recordings can be as diverse as the possibilities for auditory information that children can use.

Tape recorders permit teachers and children to develop their own resource materials. A tape recorder can be taken on a trip, for example, and the recording can be played back in class. Teachers might even take transistor recorders along on vacations, much as they do 35mm cameras today, and return with recordings instead of slides. These recordings, commercially made or teacher made, could be used by individuals or small groups if earphones are available or by the total class. Individual children can listen to recordings without disturbing the class. As a matter of fact, children would be able to make their own recordings with these devices, adding an additional medium to the area of creative expression in the kindergarten.

Similar developments in the field of photography have helped to make this communications area more useful to teachers. Kindergarten teachers have used filmstrips successfully with groups of children for a long time. There are advantages to a visual program that can unfold at a pace which can be controlled to parallel children's rate of absorption of the information. Unlike the motion picture's set speed, the pace of a filmstrip can be varied as needed, providing a great degree of flexibility to this medium. The ability to synchronize sound with filmstrips has added another useful facet to these programs. The sound can provide a narrative or other message which offers increased information or additional cues to the child. At the same time the addition of sound generally requires the viewing to proceed at a prescribed pace. In this case, flexibility is sacrificed to the advantage of additional information.

A recent development in slide projection may serve to give a comparable advantage to slide sets without the time imposition of sound filmstrips. The development of sound slides has recently been described with sound recorded on an oxide strip on the side of the slide mount, much like a magnetic tape recording. The development of sound slide programs might provide another valuable resource to the kindergarten. Filmstrips must be bought commercially because they are too expensive for teachers to develop, but slides, sound or silent, can be photographed by teachers. There are 35mm cameras today which are so automatic that they almost guarantee adequate pictures.

Slide stories developed by the teacher about different subjects can be a valuable resource. If sound is added they may become even more valuable. Projection devices have also become automatic and easy to operate. Children can view programs of slides themselves, either through a viewer or on a screen, using a nonjamming projector that simply requires focusing, flicking a switch to turn the machine on, and pressing a button in order to change the slide.

Developments in 8mm motion pictures and equipment also provide new resources to the teacher. The equipment for 8mm film, whether sound or silent, is lighter and easier to handle than the bulkier 16mm materials that are available in most schools. Sound films are now available in this medium and the equipment itself has become automated. Automatic threading devices take the dread out of film use for most teachers. Cartridge devices are available so that the 8mm silent films can be inserted on a continuous loop cartridge into the projector as easily as a slice of bread is inserted into a toaster. A single switch, operated by either a child or teacher, starts and stops the machine and allows it to be viewed by the whole class or by a single child. In this medium, materials available commercially can be supplemented by teacher or school-developed materials. Pictures can be taken and later stripped for sound if desired or left to be projected as silent films.

All of these audio-visual devices offer children sources of information that they can use, individually or in groups, in a simple and highly flexible manner. To make such devices available in the kindergarten would require an increase in the budget. Such increased costs, however, can be justified as necessary to provide efficient devices which make possible learning opportunities for young children which would not be available in any other way. The equipment itself need not be used by the kindergarten class alone. In a well administered school, a set of these mechanical devices could be shared among a large staff with careful planning for maximum use and availability.

Books

A good source of information for young children is children's books. Many well-written and beautifully illustrated books have long been available to educators of young children. In recent years excellent informational books have been published in increasing numbers. These are written especially for the young child, often under the authorship or editorship of specialists in specific areas of knowledge. The information in these books is generally accurate and up-to-date although presented in simplified form. The books are fully illustrated, and the pictures as well as the text offer usable information. Such books provide excellent sources of information to the child when they are read to him and when he is permitted to leaf through them.

Sometimes one particular child or a small group may be interested and ready for certain stories or informational books that would not be appropriate for the total class. Opportunities must be provided in these instances for individual work with books. It is not necessary for the entire class to be present every time a book is read or a story is told. During an activity period a teacher can often find opportunities to read to individuals and small groups.

Television

Television represents a powerful yet relatively untapped resource for learning on the part of young children. From very early in their lives children are exposed to television. Facts dealing with many aspects of life are available to them. All of television is not necessarily educational, and not all children learn the same amount from television; yet most children exposed to television gain some information from it. They also develop larger vocabularies through this medium, especially before age five. Television's great strength for education could be in providing the kinds of experiences that children cannot gain first-hand.

Television programs could substitute for trips to places too far away or too costly or too dangerous for children to visit. Television can bring into the classroom resource people who would not otherwise be available. Television can help children participate, however vicariously, in many activities of the culture. However, children's expectations of entertainment from television may have to be modified before good viewing habits can be established. With better programming, television can become a fine resource to help children learn more about their general environment. Control over programming is one of the important advantages of closed-circuit television, with the possibility of repeating programs and scheduling them at optimum times.

Programmed Instruction

In recent years a new field of auto-instructional education has developed. Programmed devices, either machines or books, which offer varied content to people of many different abilities and on many different levels have been forthcoming from several sources. Machines that are programmed at different degrees of complexity may offer new opportunities for the education of young children in the future. The children can work at their own pace and on their own levels with immediate knowledge of results. Machines can be developed that are simple enough for children to work, permitting self-instruction. The fact that the child can work independently at one of these devices enables the teacher to work with small groups in a class while other children are pursuing other interests and activities independently.

While auto-instructional devices are not recommended as a major learning method for young children, their possibilities for practice activities should be assessed with an open mind.

BIBLIOGRAPHY

Blough, Glenn O., and Marjorie H. Campbell, *Making and Using Classroom Science Materials in the Elementary School*, New York: Holt, Rinehart and Winston, 1954.

Dale, Edgar, *Audio-Visual Methods in Teaching* (rev. ed.), New York: Holt, Rinehart and Winston, 1954.

DeCecco, John P., *Educational Technology: Readings in Programed Instruction*, New York: Holt, Rinehart and Winston, 1964.

Hochman, Vivienne, *Trip Experiences in Early Childhood*, New York: Bank Street College of Education, 1963.

Leonard, Edith M., Dorothy Van Deman, and Lillia Miles, "Block Construction in Developing Social Concepts," in *Foundations of Learning in Childhood Education*, Columbus, Ohio: Charles E. Merrill, 1963.

Mitchell, Lucy Sprague, *Young Geographers*, New York: John Day, 1934.

Omwake, Evelyn, "The Child's Estate," in Albert J. Solnit and Sally A. Provence (Eds.), *Modern Perspectives in Child Development*, New York: International University Press, 1963, pp. 581–590.

Pratt, Caroline, *Experimental Practices in City and Country School*, New York: E. P. Dutton, 1924.

Thomas, R. Murray, and Sherman G. Swartout, *Integrated Teaching Materials: How to Choose, Create and Use Them*, New York: Longmans, Green, 1960.

8

LANGUAGE
GROWTH

Modern school education is basically symbol-oriented. While language symbols are not the only ones used and taught, they are by far the most important. Fortunately, the focus on language development even for the youngest children in school is beginning to be more deliberate and better-planned than ever before. Teachers now know that language skills can be fostered, advanced, and reinforced in many ways. Many kindergarten teachers are creative in their plans for teaching better skills of listening and speaking. Reading and writing skills are generally deferred to the first grade.

There are many reasons for helping children learn to communicate effectively. Our increasingly verbal environment and the bombardment of knowledge which children receive from all sources today require great language skill. The need to improve human relations, to help children link past and present, and to enhance their chances for success in academic and in real-life pursuits are additional urgent reasons for good language development.[1] Walcott points out that language develops as a counterpart to exploratory action, as a record of experience, and as comprehension of things discovered and the relationships of these things to other things.[2]

Although some scholars have insisted that language is not essential to thought processes, the evidence appears to support the need of

[1] Harold G. Shane, Mary E. Reddin, and Margaret C. Gillespie, *Beginning Language Arts Instruction With Children*, Columbus, Ohio: Charles E. Merrill, 1961, p. 9.

[2] Fred G. Walcott, "Language and Its Functions in Life," in Virgil E. Herrick and Leland B. Jacobs (Eds.), *Children and the Language Arts*, Englewood Cliffs, N.J.: Prentice-Hall, 1955, p. 41.

language for thought processes beyond the most primitive and concrete. Fortunately most kindergarten children enter school with good language development, an intuitive sense of good language structure, and widely varying abilities in vocabulary and language usage. Although the language tool usually exists in good form, it needs considerable practice, refinement, and development before its full potential is found. For some children the need exists for basic instruction in using language as a learning tool.

LANGUAGE IN
THE CURRICULUM

More language opportunities are needed in all kindergartens. Speech, says Langer, is the normal end-product of thought, which suggests that speech is not apart from but an essential element in the young child's thinking.[3] Words are also seen as a "focus of thought," to keep a concept in view, to prevent an idea from vanishing and having to be rediscovered.[4] A linguist suggests that simple thinking can take place without words, but not difficult or sustained thinking.[5] The need of the young child to use language to distinguish the essential features of objects, to formulate aims for constructive play as well as to verbalize the necessary means to achieve stated aims and to create imaginative play plans has been stressed by Luria, the Soviet psychologist.[6] A growing body of theory and research in the role of language in conceptual thinking supports the view that they must develop together if meanings are to be remembered and used in appropriate contexts and if progressive complexity in thinking and understanding is to take place.

Verbal communication and speaking and listening opportunities must be featured as an essential part of the kindergarten curriculum. Of course there must be periods of quiet, which are essential for

[3] Susanne K. Langer, *Philosophy in a New Key*, New York: Mentor Books, 1959, p. 48.

[4] Ernst Cassirer, *An Essay on Man: Introduction to a Philosophy of Human Culture*, Garden City, N.Y.: Doubleday, 1953, p. 171.

[5] Charlton Laird, *The Miracle of Language*, New York: Fawcett World Library, 1953, p. 224.

[6] Alexander R. Luria, *The Role of Speech in the Regulation of Normal and Abnormal Behavior*, New York: Liveright, 1961, p. 170.

listening and story-telling, as well as for receiving instructions and for rest. But the planned quiet periods should be minimal and functional for special purposes. There is no need for silence for the sake of silence in the kindergarten. Neither is there any purpose to uncontrolled bedlam. This is sometimes a reaction of children to unnecessarily long periods of quiet, to anxiety or uncertainty, and especially to inept, insecure teaching.

Most teachers recognize an optimum point of conversational buzz in the classroom which is free of shrill urgencies, relaxed and relatively uninhibited but indicates deep involvement in worthwhile pursuits. This is the point to strive for, except when quiet is required for purposes that children understand. It must be repeated that good kindergarten language programs can only grow out of stimulating experiences which are meaningful for children.

LANGUAGE OPPORTUNITIES

Language opportunities must be planned for a variety of outcomes and values. Important language opportunities to be programmed include:

1. conversation
2. perceiving and following instructions
3. formulating questions and inquiries
4. seeking information
5. expressing feelings and ideas
6. sharing information
7. listening to stories, poems, books
8. group discussion
9. creative dramatics
10. dramatic play
11. vocabulary development

Conversation

Adequate opportunities for language development through conversation will not occur without planning. It is possible to plan for sufficient conversational opportunities during the course of the day, so that these are not inadvertently omitted or relegated to snack time only. Teachers improve children's skills in conversation by example. Children can practice on toy telephones or record on tape recorders and listen to playbacks for specific skills under study. Teachers can help children focus on certain conventional forms of conversation through discussion in creative dramatics, with or without puppets. Sufficient practice opportunities under teacher guidance to improve conversational abilities is essential.

Children who use predominantly nonverbal forms of communication may be guided to more verbal and less physical responses in specific ways, through teacher suggestion. One boy in a kindergarten class tended to react with a violent punch whenever another child took a block he wanted. He was persuaded that he could achieve the desired result through courteous speech, when the teacher suggested appropriate language he could use and reminded him on several occasions. He gradually converted this previously efficient behavior to new and equally efficient verbal forms.

Conversation thrives upon challenging ideas, variety of content, and motivation and interest. One teacher in a depressed area attempted to cultivate conversation in a regular morning sharing session, when children could exchange information about anything of interest. She quickly discovered that the fabric of their lives was too threadbare. These children seldom went anywhere or did anything. Carrying on a conversation was very difficult for them in school. These children were in great need of information about the world which lay outside the narrow confines of their known community. Their lack of information was revealed when the teacher secured the use of a bus for a short trip outside of their own community. Their neighborhood abounded in tall, multiple dwellings, tenements, where people lived crowded closely in large masses. The bus took a route through a section of the city in which single one-family dwellings predominated. The children were puzzled about these buildings, speculating as to whether they were large dog houses or garages for cars. It was inconceivable to them that a house could be occupied by just one single family.

Teachers cannot assume that children come to school with the background of experiences necessary for good conversational practices. Many children will require more interesting subjects for conversation, more first-hand experiences, more understandable and absorbing ideas, before the forms of information exchange, discourse, and conversation can be improved.

Following Instructions

The ability to hear and follow instructions includes a number of skills. The cultivation of these skills is helped by the teacher's use of her voice and her determination to issue instructions only once. Additional factors are the child's interest in the material communicated, the phrasing of instructions clearly and simply, and the child's understanding of the implied or real outcomes of following or failing to follow instructions.

In many classrooms, teachers use a definite signal to convey to the children the message that instructions are about to be issued, to create a "listening set," and to give adequate warning to busy workers that their attention is being sought. Signals might include a flick of the light switch, a piano chord or holding up one hand. Once the signal is given, the teacher waits quietly for the group to perceive the signal and to get ready to listen. Finally, she talks quietly when issuing her instruction. If the class is still noisy, she takes her cue from stage actors and lowers her voice so that noise is discouraged by those straining to hear. The novice teacher tends to try to shout above the children's voices, but this usually does not help; it frequently increases the noise as children respond to the raised voice.

Teaching children to follow instructions is an important goal for the kindergarten teacher. Children who learn to follow oral instructions will be ready to learn the skills of following written instructions in workbooks and tests and real-life situations vital to their own development.

Skills in following instructions include listening, analyzing the information for clarity and logic, seeking clarification when necessary, remembering any sequence involved, and carrying out the instructions. Adults tend to forget how much of the environment is puzzling, mysterious, unclear, or unperceived by children. Children often come home from school with homework assignments that make no sense, and frequently insist that they know what the teacher said, in the face of the most logical arguments by parents that it could not have been heard accurately.

This suggests the importance of teaching children to analyze instructions to see whether they make sense. Good reading depends upon testing unknown words in this way. Children can be supported by teachers in their timid, self-conscious efforts to seek clarification. This means that the classroom must be one in which it is both acceptable and possible to obtain clarification. The teacher cannot say, "No questions! Just do as I say!" She is likely to meet with some surprises if she thinks children always understand or hear what she says.

Formulating Questions

Since formulating good questions and fruitful inquiries is difficult even for adults, young children clearly need help in developing this skill. Irrelevant questions, questions which focus on unimportant details, and poorly phrased questions which do not communicate are some of the pitfalls children can begin to become aware of. Children can be encouraged to rephrase, rethink, and re-evaluate their questions in order to state what it is they really want to know. It takes considerable sophistication to ask the right question. Knowing this, when a child asks a question, the teacher ought to take the time to uncover what the *real* question might be.

A two-and-a-half-year-old asked her mother one day what time it was. The mother automatically responded, "It's three-thirty." But then the mother wondered about the purpose of the question. Her second reaction was a more perceptive one, for the child had no conception of time but was using imitative behavior to secure her mother's attention. Any question would have served the same purpose. Children often use questions to obtain attention, rather than information. When this happens the teacher needs to study the child to learn the reasons for this behavior.

The skills of formulating good questions can be deliberately practiced along with planned, provocative, and stimulating experiences. Better questions tend to be formulated by better-informed children. Children need the opportunities to practice formulating questions so that their skills will improve as they become knowledge-able about the subject.

In the study of economic concepts referred to, children were guided to formulate a list of relevant questions before the visit to the class of a supermarket manager. In this case, the children had had about two months of study of supermarkets, and their experiences enabled them to design some really significant questions. In the class discussion, some children suggested asking the manager whether his store had meat and vegetables. This question was vetoed by the group when many children insisted that they already knew the answer from their own observations. After about ten minutes of discussion, the following questions were listed:

1. What work does the manager do?
2. What do the other people do?
3. How do you figure prices?
4. Do you have machines?
5. How does the cash register print prices on the tape?

Questions of this order of relevance would not have been formulated by this group before the accumulation of the necessary experience.

Good programs will offer opportunities for formulating questions in many situations, in explicit and socially approved ways. Sometimes the whole class can share in the formulating of inquiries, as in the example above. Sometimes, this is more fruitful in small groups or by individual children. In some cases, questions will follow an initial stimulating experience. In others the questions will come later and will serve to help the children summarize what they have learned and to point to next steps or different channels which can be explored. After a visit to an airport, children are likely to devise much more profound and significant questions, than before.

Seeking Information

If good questions and inquiries are structured, children can take steps in the direction of finding sources of information. Many young children are aware of books as sources of information only in a vague and general way. By using dictionaries, picture dictionaries, encyclopedias, and different kinds of factual books to find the information needed to answer a very specific inquiry, the teacher helps children to learn how printed sources are used for finding information. Even young children can be introduced to newspapers, periodicals, pamphlets, and special types of publications. The infinite variety of printed matter available to the consumer today offers many levels and areas of interest which can be used profitably in the kindergarten. When children have collected information, they can compose their own "books" or "newspapers," participating in the activity of preserving information in a readily accessible form for future use, which is what publications do.

Resorting to authoritative or knowledgeable adults in person for information is a regular occurrence which often saves time and energy. Children can learn to find adults who specialize in particular kinds of information and tap other sources of information. At an airport, for example, what authoritative adults can be found to answer urgent questions, and how does one find them?

Children need to learn about sources of information other than books and people. What other sources of information are there? What is available to personal observation? How do museums, zoos, art galleries, and aquariums provide information? Or photographs, slides, radio, and television? Five-year-olds cannot explore all information sources exhaustively, but they can be introduced to some of the major sources and learn their functions and values.

Information seeking requires vocabulary study and definition. Words must be used clearly and in fruitful ways. Often, new words must be introduced. Frequently, common words are used in a special way, and children's attention must be directed to multiple word meanings, content clues, and new phraseology.

Working with oral language in this way leads directly to reading for meaning. Teachers do well not to oversimplify. More is accomplished by using synonyms together with new words than by clinging only to the familiar and known word. In the geography–history study, the children used the terms "uptown" and "downtown" to designate northern and southern directions in their study of the neighborhood. Toward the end of the study the terms "north" and "south" were substituted for these directions, which had become meaningful through experiences.

Expressing Feelings and Ideas

Children, like many adults, tend to use conventional, stereotyped words and phrases, such as "cute," "terrific," and "fabulous," to express feelings and ideas. Trite and meaningless phrases can be discouraged if children have access to vocabulary sources they can use.

Good literature is an obvious source of variety in word usage and vocabulary. Stories and poems can be selected for the vivid and dramatic use of new or familiar words. Children should be encouraged to try to use new words through games, stories, and conversations.

Vocabulary and new phraseology can always be introduced with new experiences. One morning in April, a kindergarten class arrived at school in bright sunshine, laughing merrily at the snow underfoot which had fallen briefly during the night. The teacher suggested they go out immediately to the school playground, where the snow lay, free of footsteps. The children ran gaily around the yard, making patterns in the smooth white expanse of snow.

When they came indoors and removed their wraps and boots, the teacher suggested they might enjoy writing a poem about the experience in the snow and how it felt. A simple poem was recorded on newsprint paper on the easel, as the children made suggestions, line by line.

The valuable part of this experience was the process of translating fresh and vivid feelings into words, groping for communicative ones, trying to express feelings precisely, directly, by analogy, by contrast, and by pure onomatopoetic sound.

Young children do not easily recapture a mood or feeling or idea from the past. A fresh and very recent experience is usually more productive than an experience which must be recalled or re-evoked.

Sharing Information

"Show and tell," or information-sharing experiences, has come into disrepute for some very good reasons. Often these are boring, restless sessions for all but the child who happens to be speaking. Chance and irrelevant material of all sorts may be displayed by children just to have something to "show," about which they have nothing to "tell." Such sessions discourage good listening, speaking, discussion, information seeking, and the progress of any language skills. If every child in the class has to have a turn each time, this session breeds inevitable disciplinary problems by some of the less inhibited children.

This device as generally used neither promotes real communication nor contributes to children's language or conceptual development. How different is an information-sharing session which is pointed, focused, and guided! More genuine interest and community of experience and reaction results when the sharing grows out of pointed inquiry. In the economics study, the children had begun to discuss supermarkets and their functions.

A story about supermarkets was read to the children one day, and this story was used to motivate a discussion and further inquiry about such stores. The children were requested to seek some specific information over a weekend and to return to school ready to share their findings. The teacher framed a letter to all parents, read it to the class, and gave each child a copy of the letter to take home. The letter described the precise nature of the inquiry as follows:

Dear Parents:

Our class is planning to get some information about food stores. We want to find out some of the different kinds of food that are sold and some of the different kinds of jobs people do in food stores.

Your kindergartener will ask you to take him along next time there is marketing to do. By next Monday, we hope all the children will have marketed in a food store so that we can talk about it in class.

Sincerely,

Miss X
Kindergarten Teacher

The children returned the following week bursting with information, impatient to share it. They poured out much factual detail, correcting and repeating each other, embellishing details, adding color and reactive information, as well as facts. There was neither boredom nor restlessness, but deep absorption in the details of their similar experiences. This community of feeling and delight in sharing and analyzing information was even more pronounced when the whole class went to a supermarket to purchase some cookie ingredients and returned to school to discuss products on sale and workers in the store. Not only is interest greater, but it is possible to carry such discussions to greater depth, because of the shared experience. For example, in discussing the types of workers in the supermarket, one child remarked that she saw a lady getting milk, but she was immediately shouted down by a number of children, correcting the confusion of a customer with store employees.

Occasionally, a child comes to school with some new treasure, perhaps a birthday gift or an insect found on the street. Teachers should certainly encourage children to share information whenever there really is content to share.

If care is taken by the teacher to see that those items "shared" by the children have significant potentialities for learning, then such periods can serve a very worthwhile purpose. In the geography–history study, one of the children brought a bank in the shape of a globe to class to show at "sharing time." As he showed his bank to the children, a discussion of the globe ensued and the children were able to compare a flat map to a globe. In the course of a short discussion, the teacher was able to help children explore the reasons for using maps. It was pointed out that, although they are less accurate than globes, maps are more convenient.

Some teachers feel that, if every child is not required to take a turn at sharing, the shy and timid ones will never have the experience of talking to a group. However, these children could be encouraged to participate actively in some of the challenging experiences available in the classroom, to stimulate the desire and encourage the ability to communicate. All children need this kind of language experience. Some children find little material for this at home. For such children, the school must provide the excitement, novelty, and drama of activities worth talking about.

Listening Activities

Sometimes listening is compulsory and sometimes it is not. If teachers will make such distinctions explicit and deliberate, even five-year-olds can quickly become better listeners.

Instructions for a fire-alarm drill or for beginning a new total class activity are compulsory. Everyone is required to listen, and listening is featured as the sole legitimate activity at such times. But such intense listening can be neither demanded nor expected at all times. Adults know very well how quickly they can resort to daydreams or reveries to avoid listening to anything they would rather not hear. Children have the same weapons at their disposal and less conscience to inhibit their employment.

Much classroom listening must be placed in the voluntary category. Listening to books, stories, poems, records, comments, and contributions by the teacher or other children seems to require a strong element of volition for success. How can we fail to tune out a monotonous teacher's voice or a whining child's voice, an unpleasant, scratched quality on a record, or simply any topic which bores or fails to interest us, no matter how communicated? Requiring children to listen to everything, whether they wish to or not, only cultivates nonlistening habits of inattention. Children learn to assume blank faces to hide their inattention or their inner concentration on anything else.

Therefore, required listening should be kept to the barest minimum. When it is necessary, it should be so indicated. Required listening can be given greater urgency and appeal by its infrequency, its brevity, its intrinsic importance or interest, and by the teacher's sincerity in conveying whatever she needs to communicate. Required listening can be further distinguished by the absence of alternative activities.

When listening is voluntary, no stigma attaches to the nonlistener. The story, book, record, radio, or television program is not expected to appeal to everyone. Or, perhaps it is not expected to appeal to everyone at the same time. There are a few children who listen very intently to music on records and who find even the presence of other quiet children distracting. Some children only enjoy a story which a teacher reads to a very small group of children, enjoying not only the quiet reading but the intimacy, identity, sense of belonging, and close contact with the small group.

Children's listening skills may improve dramatically when they have a voice in selecting, deciding, or planning the material to be heard. This is often true, even when the choice is between only two alternatives.

New kindergarten teachers often despair of ever attaining a satisfying, quiet, listening class at story-time. Yet, this is easily accomplished if children help to choose the story and if those children who do not wish to listen are permitted to do something else. Story time is not the time for unlimited choice of alternatives, since other noises disrupt the story. But there are many fairly quiet activities in any classroom, such as puzzles picture cards, books, table toys, and crayons which can be ready, to use. Teachers who offer alternatives often find that they achieve total-class listening indirectly this way. Many children are quite willing to listen provided that their hands are busy. Sitting with hands folded is just too difficult for some young children. Cultivating listening habits enables children to hear much that really interests them. Ultimately the intrinsic interest of the material motivates voluntary listening.

When listening seems unpopular, and too many children prefer to do something else, the teacher needs to become as objective as she can to analyze the contributing factors and to plan for improvement. She can record her own voice on a tape recorder, reading or speaking, to discover a need for improvement in voice use. She can discuss listening activities with the children, seeking information from them as to elements that seem to detract from the holding power of such experiences. Analysis of her programming will help her to discover whether the sequence, timing or other factors should be changed. She can analyze the material which is being used for its interest for the children in the class. Sometimes novelty or surprise stimulates renewed interest. Pictures, puppets, a flannel board, or other props are available for this purpose.

Group Discussions

Group discussions can become important opportunities for practicing skills of listening, thinking, and communicating. These are intensely social experiences for young children and are therefore dependent upon children's social controls and maturity for success. Teacher guidance of the discussion is essential to establish a classroom climate conducive to orderly exchange and to establish standards of behavior.

Sometimes teachers plan a total-class discussion which they expect to carry on for fifteen or twenty minutes, but which they cut short because of restlessness and lack of interest after five minutes. At other times, interest runs so high that the discussion goes on for forty-five minutes before the teacher notices the time and brings the discussion to a close, in order to fit in other routines. If teachers can be this flexible and sensitive to children's day-by-day behavior variations, the discussion skills of the class are likely to develop rapidly, because they are not cut short when good discussions are in progress, but are quickly terminated when the day or hour does not seem propitious. Children are more likely to begin to enjoy their discussion sessions and therefore to improve their discussion skills.

Successful progress in discussion skills, however, is also closely linked with the intrinsic interest of the material discussed and with the teacher's ability to integrate this with interesting, significant, and exciting classroom projects. Frequent discussions make discussion rules more understandable, more frequently practiced, and better understood. The extent of group involvement is another important element. A topic which is one of common interest to the group or about which there have been common experiences is likely to engender better discussion than a topic about which few children have either information or experience.

Maintenance of friendly, orderly procedures, without undue tension, contributes substantially to good discussion sessions. For this, the teacher needs good humor, patience, and good interpersonal relationships.

Creative Dramatics

Creative dramatics is a more deliberate, planned, and structured form of role playing than dramatic play, which is completely improvised by the children. There are some excellent books on creative dramatics suggesting standards for selection of stories and roles, ways to make young children aware of characterization and projection of character traits, of story sequences and incidents to be portrayed, of mood, atmosphere, and finer nuances of feeling.[7] This

[7] See especially Winifred Ward, *Playmaking with Children*, New York: Appleton-Century-Crofts, 1959; Pamela P. Walker, *Seven Steps to Creative Dramatics*, New York: Hill and Wang, 1957; Frances C. Durland, *Creative Dramatics for Children*, Yellow Springs, Ohio: Antioch Press, 1952; and Margaret S. Woods, *Creative Dramatics*, Washington, D.C.: National Education Association, 1959.

delightful mode of organization and communication of ideas can be used with five-year-olds to further language and conceptual progress.

In a typical creative dramatics program, the teacher selects some story which the children know very well, such as "The Gingerbread Man," or she permits the children to assist in selecting an appropriate story. The story is discussed so that the narration helps the children recall the sequence of events and the cast of characters. Parts are cast, from volunteers, by teacher-selection, by lots, or by class vote. Before the children start to play their parts, there is usually further discussion about the characteristics of each part and ways of portraying it, the number of incidents or scenes to be shown and the action to be included in each.

> For example, a group of five-year-olds loved the story of "The Gingerbread Man" and had requested it several times in one week. The teacher had carefully prepared the telling of the story, using simple construction paper cut-outs of the characters to heighten interest and meaning. The children enjoyed chanting the refrain: "Run, run, as fast as you can, you can't catch me, I'm the Gingerbread Man!"
>
> The teacher suggested one morning that the children might enjoy acting out the story, discussed the story briefly with the children, listed the characters and asked for volunteers for the parts. She pinned character names on the children's blouses, so that she could remember the cast and then asked the children to summarize the sequence of events. After this, she turned to each actor and discussed his part, inviting comments from the whole group on such questions as how would the old woman walk, what would she wear, what would she be doing. The group entered into this discussion with zest, making suggestions, and acting out some of the suggested business or behavior.
>
> The teacher had prepared a few simple pieces of costuming: an apron, a scarf, a pot, and a spoon for the old woman; long sticks as hoes for the farmers; and construction-paper ears or tails for the various animal characters. The children donned their costumes and galloped through the play at great speed, reminding each other whose turn it was, what action was planned, or what the character was supposed to say.
>
> After the play, the teacher asked the children to evaluate their own performances, to suggest additional ways of projecting the action or character and ways of improving the play. These suggestions were numerous, after the teacher began to ask, "How else could the old

woman show she was old?" and similar questions. Other children wanted turns to do the play and it was agreed that it would be done again the next day with a different cast.

Using new words in context, in active play or manipulation and in conjunction with a synonym gives children enough meaning clues so that they can begin to understand the word and to use it correctly themselves. In the above example, the word "ingredients" could have been used, in discussing what foods the old woman needed to bake gingerbread cookies, the word "utensils" could have been used in discussing what kinds of pots, pans, and cutlery the old woman needed for her baking, and the word "aroma" or "fragrance" or both could be introduced in connection with the smell of baking cookies. The teacher must find occasions to repeat the word and the word clues, until it is caught up in classroom usage. Pictures are additional helpful clues to meaning.

Creative dramatics is a happy choice for playing historical episodes. Teachers who despair of communicating meaning about George Washington or Christopher Columbus could use this form to integrate learnings which may have been collected in a variety of other ways. This is creative because lines are not memorized and are seldom the same twice. Instead, children use their own words to convey meanings. The emphasis is on recalling the sequence of events, the nature of the characters involved and the meaning of the dramatic action devised.

As a way of synthesizing learnings and verbalizing new under-standings, creative dramatics can be an excellent medium. The content does not have to be a fanciful tale, but can be derived from historic incidents, social situations, or other informational sources. Creative dramatic reconstructions of historical events revolving around national holidays can help children to recreate elements of the past. When children bring in historical material from such sources as movies or television, the teacher can base creative dramatic activities on these.

The supermarket project could have been dramatized as children made progress in their concept development. The roles that were played by the children in dramatic play were generally limited to storekeeper and customer. Using the creative dramatic technique, other roles could have been explored, such as stockman, checker, butcher, produce man, and manager. These roles were not unknown to the children, but they did not explore them in play.

Dramatic Play

When children decide to play house and one of them casts herself as the mother while others take similar appropriate roles, this is dramatic play. The endless versions of "cops and robbers" played by kindergarten boys, whether as Superman, Mighty Mouse, or astronauts, constitute versions of dramatic play.

Omwake differentiates between the spontaneous play of children and structured play. The former includes most of the dramatic play found in nursery schools. The latter is differentiated by the degree of control the teacher imposes on the activity, determining time, place, and materials, as well as setting the limits of play activities. Both are seen as meeting the educational needs of young children. Omwake goes on to suggest that play can be used to diagnose learning difficulties in children, and to prevent learning problems from occurring. The teacher can help children overcome learning problems through "play tutoring," or "remedial play teaching," where she offers specific help to individual children through play situations.[8]

While this form of play is essentially impulsive there are a number of ways in which such play can be guided to support intellectual learning. Ways to influence dramatic play include planning settings, changing settings, supplying specific types of equipment, props, and costumes, and making explicit suggestions. Even more fundamental is the programming of content and experiences which will tempt children to use dramatic play as one way of practicing learning and integrating classroom experiences of different kinds. Children can subsequently describe, evaluate, and analyze their dramatic play activities, with the teacher's guidance, to develop more sophisticated play.

Every time the teacher reads a book, shows a picture, or provides

[8] Evelyn B. Omwake, "The Child's Estate," in Albert J. Solnit and Sally A. Provence (Eds.), *Modern Perspectives in Child Development*, New York: International Universities Press, 1963, pp. 581–590.

any sort of experience to children, she is influencing dramatic play. Her selection or rejection of any specific piece of equipment for the classroom and her determination of its use affects dramatic play. The kinds of costumes, props, and accessories she provides similarly structures dramatic play. Since teaching necessarily structures children's activities, the real decision the teacher makes is the determination of the direction and purpose of dramatic play.

Lengths of wire and sundry hardware items with a tool chest frequently suggest roles of various kinds of skilled repairmen; boys, and even some girls, will be delighted to play such roles. Other roles teachers can suggest to children include those of policemen, mailmen, storekeepers and customers, bus and truck drivers, ship's captains and airline pilots, radio and television announcers or newscasters, scientists, and any other roles which the teacher has planned to illuminate in some meaningful way for the group. Playing these roles produces little learning in and of itself, but any of these could be productive in helping children make their understandings explicit and concrete, in synthesizing, analyzing, and seeking patterns in their information which may point to principles, rules, generalizations, and abstractions. The teacher's active and perceptive guidance of the play may result in substantial conceptual growth.

Another way to motivate the playing of roles is through the use of puppets. Some classrooms have a collection of hand-puppets which children readily use, adopting voice tones, language, and action regarded as suitable for the specific character. Five-year-olds can also make very simple stick puppets, which are usually cut-outs pasted or stapled to a tongue-depressor. The cut-out may be the child's own drawing or a clipping from a magazine or other source.

More elaborate puppets can be made by the teacher and by many children using papier-mâché, cutting and sewing socks into desired shapes, or by using other materials. Some puppets have no strong, obvious characteristics or occupations, and children use these simply to get into any other role they have in mind. Some puppets are made very distinctive, as firemen or sailors, and dictate the part to be played. But any child can dominate a puppet and play any character his way, which is clearly one of the great assets puppets have in the classroom.

Teachers, hearing the language children use in role-playing, use this information diagnostically, to plan for ways to effect needed progress. Teachers' questions can provoke and stimulate more sophisticated play. If children play house, and the mother and father play they are always "at home," the teacher's questions can relate to what errands a mother has to do, where she may have to go on occasion, what meetings she attends, what job the father has, when he is at home, when he is away, etc. Increasingly searching questions often serve to remind children of information they already have but sometimes it serves to initiate some new inquiry, to find new information. It may impel them to observe more closely and to interpret more meaningfully what they see. Teacher guidance can help children to integrate their information so that they can play more complex roles.

Books and Printed Materials

It has been noted that in our increasingly aural world, so much dominated by radio, television, loudspeakers, telephones, and other means of oral communication, a surprising number of homes lack books or other printed materials. The kindergarten child's strongest motivation to learn to read can come from his intense desire to obtain information and enjoyment from the printed page which he observes in adults. The less motivation of this kind in the home, the greater need there is to stimulate it through the kindergarten teacher's use of books and other reading materials.

Kindergarten classroom libraries are essential but most of them are quite inadequate in number of volumes and in the range of content represented. Kindergarten teachers often find ways to supplement these inadequate collections—with books borrowed from public libraries, from children in the class, and from other classrooms, with donations and gifts from the PTA, and through other means. Many children like to bring personally owned books to school, and, when the content is appropriate, these can be read to the class. Kindergarten budgets should provide for not just a few of the best new trade books each year, but also picture dictionaries, an adult dictionary, and such other reference materials as the teacher may require. The school library should, of course, have several of the best encyclopedias.

Other printed materials which could be used in the classroom include:

1. Magazines and newspapers, especially Sunday magazine supplements.
2. Posters, of which there are many now available from educational publishers focusing on ideas and concepts.
3. Maps, pictures and photographs with or without texts, atlases, and almanacs.
4. Pamphlets, especially those with illustrations or those with good texts which the teacher can read to interested children.
5. Much free material available from commercial advertisers, when the content is relevant.

Children often demand that teachers read picture captions and surrounding texts when the pictures are attractive or provocative. Some teachers feature the utility of reading by reading recipes, when a cooking experience is in order, by reading instructions for the use of equipment in the classroom, by reading street signs as the class goes on a trip, by reading notices which are being sent home to parents, or by reading school rules and regulations. When children help to compose a letter, story, or book, the relationship between spoken language and written symbols seems more immediate and visible and children remember and understand better material which incorporates their own language. This is, of course, one of the important reasons for using children's experiences for charts for beginning reading.

Some children have never owned their own books and have therefore missed a source of enjoyment that is commonplace for many other children and adults. Since there are so many inexpensive books available for purchase today, when teachers discover a lack of book-ownership among pupils, steps can be taken to overcome this. Sometimes, teachers can make suggestions to parents for book purchasing, but there are times when she hesitates to do this, if she knows there is a large family dependent upon a small income. Sometimes, the teacher can encourage children to bank pennies in a classroom "bank," saving them so that when a book fair is held at the school, every child has enough money to purchase one of the inexpensive little books. Not only is pride in book ownership thus encouraged but often good habits of book handling and care as well.

Teaching Reading

The place of reading in the kindergarten is currently the topic of various research projects which may contribute a better understanding of some of the controversial questions at issue.

Teachers will be interested in the research on early readers by Durkin, which so far has failed to find any disadvantages traceable to the child's having learned to read at home prior to entrance into first grade.[9] A longitudinal study of the progress of these early readers in school is under way. These studies do not throw light on reading instruction in the kindergarten class at school. Other studies now in progress on teaching reading in the kindergarten may add new insight.

Kindergarten teachers rarely discover that an occasional child has learned to read at home. Somehow, it never comes up! Even first-grade teachers tend to assume that all children are at the same nonreading level, and they proceed with "readiness" activities without discovering that one or two children are already reading at the second- or third-grade level. Better evaluation techniques in the kindergarten and at the beginning of the first grade should prevent such oversight.

The teaching of reading is often suggested as a solution to the problem of lack of significant content in the kindergarten. However, reading as a subject should not be introduced into the kindergarten for want of anything better. As has been indicated in this chapter, there are many essential language learnings which require the careful attention of kindergarten teachers and which must be attained by five-year-olds before launching into the process of learning to read.

Concern for the individual differences within any class, however, requires the teacher to consider the teaching of reading when appropriate. The most fruitful forms for such instruction have yet to be discovered but must clearly differ from those of the primary grades. Although parental concerns and pressures must be dealt with in satisfactory ways, these should not be decisive in the resolution of this problem. The problems of teacher flexibility and

[9] Dolores Durkin, "Children Who Learned to Read at Home," *Elementary School Journal*, 1961 (Oct.), 62:14–18.

adaptability to the learning needs of each individual child are not unique to this particular area.

Difficult and as yet little-researched problems concern what should be the nature of kindergarten reading instruction: Must it be entirely individualized, or is some grouping possible? What content can be used? How can the reading be integrated with the rest of the program, and how can first-grade content articulate with such kindergarten instruction? Other thorny problems relate to parental concerns and pressures on children who may not be ready for reading instruction.

BIBLIOGRAPHY

Cassirer, Ernst, *An Essay on Man: Introduction to a Philosophy of Human Culture*, Garden City, N.Y.: Doubleday, 1953.

Durkin, Dolores, "Children Who Learned to Read at Home," *Elementary School Journal*, 1961 (Oct.), 62:14–18.

Durland, Frances C., *Creative Dramatics for Children*, Yellow Springs, Ohio: Antioch Press, 1952.

Herrick, Virgil E., and Leland B. Jacobs (Eds.), *Children and the Language Arts*, Englewood Cliffs, N.J.: Prentice-Hall, 1955.

Laird, Charlton, *The Miracle of Language*, New York: Fawcett World Library, 1953.

Larrick, Nancy, *A Teacher's Guide to Children's Books*, Columbus, Ohio: Charles E. Merrill, 1960.

Langer, Susanne K., *Philosophy in a New Key*, New York: Mentor Books, 1959.

Loban, Walter D., *The Language of Elementary School Children*, Champaign, Ill.: National Council of Teachers of English, 1963.

Luria, Alexander R., *The Role of Speech in the Regulation of Normal and Abnormal Behavior*, New York: Liveright, 1961.

———, and Ia. Yudovich, *Speech and the Development of Mental Processes in the Child, An Experimental Investigation* (edited by Joan Simon), London: Staples Press, 1959.

Monroe, Marion, and Bernice Rogers, *Foundations for Reading, Informal Pre-Reading Procedures*, Chicago: Scott Foresman, 1964.

Omwake, Evelyn B., "The Child's Estate," in Albert J. Solnit and Sally A. Provence (Eds.), *Modern Perspectives in Child Development*, New York: International Universities Press, 1963, pp. 581–590.

Shane, Harold G., Mary E. Reddin, and Margaret C. Gillespie, *Beginning Language Arts Instruction with Children*, Columbus, Ohio: Charles E. Merrill, 1961.

Walcott, Fred G., "Language and Its Functions in Life," in Virgil E.

Herrick and Leland B. Jacobs (Eds.), *Children and the Language Arts*, Englewood Cliffs, N. J.: Prentice-Hall, 1955.

Walker, Pamela P., *Seven Steps to Creative Dramatics*, New York: Hill and Wang, 1957.

Ward, Winifred, *Playmaking with Children*, New York: Appleton-Century-Crofts, 1959.

Woods, Margaret S., *Creative Dramatics*, Washington, D.C.: National Education Association, 1959.

9

EVALUATION AND CONCLUSIONS

The development of an evaluation design is an important part of any good program. The more clearly the teacher can express the goals of the program, the more precisely she can appraise the results. Evaluating the program by pinpointing its strengths and deficits provides the specific kind of information needed for an improved curriculum.

Evaluation is a judgment-making process by which the teacher gathers and organizes information, weighs evidence, makes inferences, and reaches decisions. Evaluation improves with increased knowledge of the variety of tools available, judicious selection of appropriate ones, and a realization of the limitations of all evaluative techniques. The major methods teachers can use for gaining information are observations of children's behavior and tests. While there are other sources of information, such as children's products and projective devices, these are not as likely to produce information helpful to the teacher in evaluating conceptual progress. The main purpose in accumulating data is to help teachers make judgments about children's learning and about the results of the program so that these decisions will be translated into action which results in improved programs and increased learning.

Teachers may need assistance in initiating some programs of evaluation and should be able to receive the same kind of expert help which is available in other school evaluation procedures. Teacher self-improvement may occur whenever the data can help the teacher to determine the kinds of change needed in teaching for greater effectiveness and for children's continuous progress in learning. The evaluation may also furnish some important clues to the inadequacies of the planned curriculum and the direction of needed change.

PLANNING
EVALUATION

Ideally, evaluation should be part of the planning which precedes the initiation of a program in a classroom. Advance planning contributes to a balanced program of evaluation, to clarification of objectives, and to superior construction of evaluative devices. However, some instruments grow out of intuition, insights, hunches, and teachers' understandings of a "hindsight" character which promise better techniques next time. When teachers see a new way to obtain more meaningful evaluation, they should exericse the same flexibility they would use in other areas of the program. Evaluation of conceptual learning requires first a statement of goals or desired concepts to be developed. Secondly, these goals must be translated into a concise statement of either desired behavioral outcomes or understandings which can be achieved by five-year-olds. If the goals can be spelled out in terms of observable behavior, the teacher will be more apt to collect information about their attainment by the children. These outcomes, then, become the *what* of the evaluation program.

The *how* of evaluation of conceptual progress concerns the determination of efficient and fruitful ways to appraise children's learning and their ability to understand and use the concepts selected. The teacher may also wish to evaluate the extent of transfer or generalization of good thinking skills, such as the ability to define or generalize or think logically.

Standardized tests are not yet available for evaluating conceptual learning in the kindergarten. Desirable as such tests are, however, they do not replace the many devices the teacher can develop in the classroom. As children gather information and put it to use, the teacher can gauge not only the specific details they have acquired but also what meaning this has for them, what significant relationships they have begun to comprehend and whether they are able to apply new understandings in unfamiliar contexts. Teachers may find it useful to look at some ways of classifying cognitive levels before planning their programs of evaluation.[1] However, there is increasing interest in the development of tests to evaluate children's conceptual learning, especially in programs designed to offer compensatory education to disadvantaged young children. Teachers may find it helpful to keep abreast of the professional literature where new developments are first reported.

For most teaching purposes suggested in this book, it will be assumed that the teacher is seeking ways to evaluate learning of specific concepts with which children are dealing in the classroom. It should be stressed that all evaluative techniques are methods of sampling behavior and therefore it is generally better to obtain several samples than only one, for greater reliability. It is also preferable to use more than one evaluative method for cross-checking. Where possible, greater objectivity can be attained when more than one person evaluates the results independently. Nonstandardized test methods generally permit more frequent evaluation as well as appraisal of qualities which are not covered by standardized tests. Readers are urged to consult some of the excellent books on educational evaluation listed in the bibliography for more detailed information.

Observational Techniques

Teachers "know" most of what they learn about children from observing them. Teachers generally note what goes on without keeping records simply because they are very busy and because they are not looking for specific kinds of behavior. Unfocused observation can defeat many good recording intentions.

When teachers have selected specific concepts to develop with children, they know what they are looking for and their observations can be focused sharply on behavioral evidence relating to such concepts. For example, in both the geography–history and economics studies, observers received instructions as to what to record in the classroom. They were furnished with a list of the understandings

[1] Benjamin S. Bloom (Ed.), *Taxonomy of Educational Objectives: The Classification of Educational Goals*, Handbook I: Cognitive Domain, New York: David McKay, 1956.

which it was hoped children would learn and were instructed to record classroom occurrences and conversations relevant to these concepts. The observers, who took turns recording, were further cautioned not to interpret events but to record them as accurately as possible, to be satisfied with summarizing episodes which could not be recorded in detail because of rapidity of dialogue or of actions, in short, to make running notes or summaries of actions and conversations which were related to the specified concepts. In the economics study, most of the play and activity concerning the concepts under study tended to take place in a rather small, confined area which had been designed to represent a store, though sometimes the activity was confined to table play if a game were in process or a book was being read to a small group. In the geography–history study, activity was less localized and occurred in several areas, including the blocks, art tables, and the outdoor play area.

In most classrooms, the activity concerning work with specified concepts would tend to be concentrated in some part of the room because of the use of some special kind of equipment or materials. Teachers are unable to take the time to write running notes or verbatim reports, but they are able to jot down key words and abbreviations on cards to remind them of the details needed for writing anecdotal records when time permits. When a group or total class discussion occurs, the teacher can make brief summaries later, as soon as the opportunity presents itself. Tape recordings of discussions will provide verbatim records which can be analyzed at the teacher's convenience. There are several helpful guides to teachers for writing anecdotal records.[2] The most important guidelines are: recording behavior without judgmental assessment, selecting relevant behavior to record, collecting sufficient anecdotal records over a period of time so that some patterns emerge, appraising these

[2] See Dorothy H. Cohen and Virginia Stern, *Observing and Recording the Behavior of Young Children*, New York: Teachers College Press, Teachers College, Columbia University, 1958; Millie Almy, *Ways of Studying Children*, New York: Teachers College Press, Teachers College, Columbia University, 1959; R. Murray Thomas, *Judging Student Progress*, New York: Longmans, Green, 1960; J. Wayne Wrightstone, Joseph Justman, and Irving Robbins, *Evaluation in Modern Education*, New York: American Book, 1956; and Robert L. Thorndike and Elizabeth Hagen, *Measurement and Evaluation in Psychology and Education* (2nd ed.), New York: John Wiley and Sons, 1961.

records, checking these records against collateral evidence, and making balanced evaluations.

Omitting judgmental assessment means describing the child's behavior objectively. For example, recording a judgment, such as "Tom is a very confused little boy," is neither informative nor capable of providing comparison with other recordings. To be really useful, the recording could describe the nature of Tom's confusion, such as, "Tom, who had been playing storekeeper during the work period, described his role as that of a customer during the group discussion which followed." The statement of the facts furnishes the teacher with the basis for working with Tom to clarify his understandings and for comparison with future observations to determine whether Tom succeeds in gaining the distinction between these two roles.

To pursue this example further, the teacher would be guided in her selection of relevant behavior to record by the concepts which she wants the class to learn, as well by the play situations in which individual children are engaged which are related to specific concepts. The teacher might want to question Tom about his role-playing, to see whether he really understands more than he seemed to. Some children become confused when they are communicating with a whole class but can be clear and cogent alone with the teacher. The teacher would also want to find additional instances of Tom's role-playing in store play, to see whether he begins to be clearer about the different roles involved.

Teachers must guard against generalizing about children's behavior from only one or two instances. Over a period of time, when samples of behavior begin to confirm a particular hypothesis or to define behavior clearly, the teacher can feel more secure in reaching conclusions. Sometimes, a series of recordings do not support any conclusion except the need for further information.

When the teacher has collected records in sufficient quantity to furnish helpful information, she needs to study this information, to make comparisons and contrasts, sometimes to classify information so that comparison is facilitated. It may sometimes be productive to grade the quality of thinking evidenced by different recordings or to grade the level of understanding reached by different children at different times. Needless to say, these are not grades for report cards; this is simply one way for the teacher to compare conceptual growth among the children in a group or to compare one child's growth over a period of time. Teachers will find it helpful to check such appraisals against any collateral evidence they may have, such as birth dates, medical records, and information from nursery schools, day care centers, and any psychological tests which may have been administered. Making a balanced evaluation requires relating different kinds of pertinent information, allowing for any shortcomings in the records, such as a small proportion of recordings for one child because of his high absence rate or for any other reason, and maintaining a tentative point of view about the results.

A kindergarten teacher is seldom able to check her own observations against those of other trained adults, but this is sometimes possible when she has a student teacher, when two teachers work together, or when an assistant teacher is provided. Since most teachers will have to rely upon their own observations, they will need to be systematic in accumulating records. They will need to schedule observations in order to obtain an adequate sample of every child's behavior in a variety of situations spaced over periods of time, so that any changes will be reflected in the data gathered. Some teachers enter children's names on cards and regularly draw three or four cards each day, to remind them to focus on specific children and to record some behavior samples for each child.

Systematic collection of observational material can be facilitated by the use of checklists, rating scales, time samplings, charts, observation guides, and other forms.

Checklists and Rating Scales

Both checklists and rating scales are limited to the evaluation of visible and readily ascertained qualities. Simple checklists can be set up to mark progress or achievement levels in regard to specific concepts. For example, in the economics study, when children were playing a game involving the identification of coins, a simple list could have been set up under a set of headings such as that in Checklist 1. Or, instead of recording Y's and N's, the teacher could

Checklist 1

Name of Child	Can Identify (Y for Yes and N for No)				
	pennies	nickels	dimes	quarters	half-dollars

simply check the columns in which the child had shown success, leaving blank the rest. If these checklists were to be used more than once, to determine progress, space could be left after each child's name for the number of additional observations planned. This form or checklist could be set up in different ways, depending upon the teacher's decision of how she will use it.

In some classrooms, teachers ask children to check their own names on a list which she posts in a convenient spot on the wall. For example, children who play in the block area are asked to check their names each day they play with blocks, furnishing the teacher with an easily recorded form of valuable information as to which children frequently, rarely, or never play with blocks. Similar lists can be posted for the use of any other materials in the classroom.

Rating scales permit the recording of degrees or levels of achievement or performance. The record can be made using the numbers "1," "2," and "3"; terms to indicate degree, such as "always," "usually," "seldom," and "never"; the qualitative terms seen on report cards: "excellent," "good," "fair," "poor," and "unsatisfactory"; or descriptive terms, such as, "has only played one role in store play, that of the customer." The teacher can simplify record keeping by developing her own code, using numbers, letters, or other symbols.

Rating scales require a judgment to be made at the time of recording and should therefore require the recording of only such judgments as can be made readily and objectively. The traits to be evaluated should be selected with care, not only as to their ease of rating but also as to the significance of the item rated. The teacher always has to decide whether the information which she can obtain so readily by these methods is worth having, whether it contributes anything worthwhile to her evaluation. Checklists and rating scales can be compiled with ease and speed for the whole class, providing comparability and complete coverage, and these can be compared at different times, to note changes and progress.

Time sampling, or the observation of a specific child's behavior at regular time intervals, is also limited to readily observed behavior. It has the additional quality of greater reliability because of the sampling technique, avoiding the recording of only isolated incidents. For example, a teacher may have the impression that a certain child does not recognize number numerals because she noted one situation in which he did not seem to know them. Instead of relying on this isolated and onetime sample, the teacher might resolve to find ways to observe this child's understanding of number symbols, every hour on the hour, in situations in which he would be responding to numerals. She might decide to assign numbers to children on some days, to indicate turns for various purposes, perhaps to work with some highly prized new piece of equipment or to take notes to the office or for other purposes. The result of time sampling is a series of observations, instead of only one on a given day, spaced according to some predetermined scale: hourly, half-hourly, or any other way. Taking a series of planned observations assures a better sample of the child's usual behavior.

Observation guides can be very useful to focus on specific kinds of behavior by listing them. The same observation guide can be used over periods of time. Teachers can develop observation guides for many different purposes, changing them as needed. Such a guide specifies certain kinds of behavior to be observed and to be recorded, using a simple symbol, such as a checkmark or an "X."

For example, teachers can develop observation guides for collecting information about children's progress in learning or using concepts in mathematics. A teacher could use a guide such as the one in Checklist 2, if she structures situations in which she can observe children's ability to use number concepts, such as in finding out how many juice cups and cookies are needed at snack time, or how many blocks of different types there are, or in ascertaining quantities of beads, cubes, or other objects.

When children engage in self-selected activities during their work periods, a wealth of observational material is available to the teacher, if she has found some useful forms in which to record and preserve

Checklist 2

Concepts	Names of Children						
	Mary	Ellen	John	Joseph	Marla	Jane	Jill
Rational counting:							
a. to 5							
b. to 10							
c. to 15							
d. to 20							
e. over 20							
Grouping sets:							
a. of 2							
b. of 3							
c. of 4							
d. of 5							
e. larger sets							
Order of counting numbers:							
a. to 5							
b. to 10							
c. to 15							
d. to 20							
e. over 20							
Recognition of numerals:							
a. to 5							
b. to 10							
c. to 15							
d. to 20							
e. over 20							

these observations for purposes of evaluation. Teachers are not limited, however, to recording free and unstructured play situations. Rich and informative as these are, they often fail to yield the kind of information which the teacher may require, or comparable information for all the children. In the geography–history study, one group discussion centered on the purpose of the dock in a harbor, eliciting a variety of responses on various intellectual levels, some more logical than others. Asking children to respond, individually or as a group, to a question becomes an oral test situation which furnishes useful comparative data on most of the children in the group. While children in groups have some tendency to repeat each other's responses, they have less inhibition in maintaining contrary points of view at five years of age than at later stages in their development.

Sometimes it is possible to tape record a classroom experience, to be studied and analyzed in depth at a later time. Tape recordings are often difficult to secure because of extraneous noise, the softness of children's voices, the difficulty of identifying speakers later, and problems of keeping speakers close enough to the microphone. In some situations, this is the ideal method of recording observations for accuracy, preservation of original voices and intonations and the opportunity for other personnel to hear the recording at a later date, with unparalleled opportunities for restudy and reinterpretation.

A teacher's conversation, or oral interview or test with one child, or with a group of children, can be recorded in this way. Studying such recordings helps the teacher to realize how selective and unreliable one's memory can be, and how much of verbal interaction can be missed, because of one's failure to hear, observe, or immediately comprehend all that is going on. Perhaps the classroom of the future will be equipped with transparent soundproof booths for tape recording and for listening activities as well.

Tests

There are some standardized tests which are designed to measure certain kinds of conceptual ability which teachers are generally not trained to administer and interpret. There are also many kinds of "readiness" tests with which teachers are familiar and which are regularly administered in many kindergartens. Many tests depend heavily upon verbal ability and tend to discriminate against children from culturally different backgrounds. While standardized tests have a place in a balanced program of evaluation, teachers may wish considerable assistance from expert personnel on the school staff before selecting, administering or interpreting such tests.

The authors of this book found it necessary to evolve their own tests in order to evaluate children's progress in learning the concepts developed in each study. While the tests have considerable differences, they both relied on oral test interviews with individual children, they were both pretested on other children and they both used a variety of test techniques, including direct questions, requesting responses to pictures and to objects. In both tests the researcher recorded the test results himself. In the geography–history study, the results were also electronically recorded. In the economics study, a large proportion of responses called for were of a nonverbal or performance type, to minimize five-year-old problems with language.

It must be granted that testing young children, even under optimum conditions, involves difficult problems, which Jersild has summarized as follows:

> When children respond to tests of their reasoning ability, many factors other than "pure reason" come into play. One child may be interested in one problem but bored by a second. Another child may be challenged by almost any kind of questioning. One youngster may feel that he ought to come up with some kind of answer while another is more free simply to say that he doesn't know. One youngster may try to face the problem that is put to him directly, another may try to figure out what the adult questioner has in mind. A youngster may give a straightforward response or answer with his tongue in cheek—offering any answer that comes to mind because he thinks he should have some sort of reply or persisting in an answer even if he has doubts about it.[3]

In addition to the problems Jersild has listed in testing young children, there is the one encountered when testing children who lack test sophistication. Although five-year-olds generally have no test experience, middle-class children usually are prepared to respond to adults and to anticipate their expectations. Within the give-and-take of their family interaction are many of the elements of the test situation, including responding to questioning and probing and interacting with a wide circle of adults. Teachers who teach children in lower socio-economic groups will have to be aware of the need to develop test-taking skills before testing begins. This simply means trial test situations of sufficient number and variety that the

[3] Arthur T. Jersild, *Child Psychology* (5th ed.), Englewood Cliffs, N.J.: Prentice-Hall, 1960, p. 361.

children come to understand how to respond and what is expected of them.

Sometimes there are difficulties in securing a good physical setting for testing, including privacy, comfort, freedom from interruption, and lack of distracting noises. All of these difficulties must be regarded as possible sources of test limitations so that teachers who give tests must be ready to appraise their usefulness in the light of all their limitations.

Having pointed to the many sources of problems in administering and interpreting tests, we must add that, if the tests probe significant learnings and understandings, rather than the superficial and readily seen qualities which may be more easily ascertained, the testing may still be the most valuable, or the most efficient way to accomplish this. Teachers can be very experimental in devising and using such tests and evaluating the results against the sources of error. As teachers modify and change tests, based on experience with them, more valid and reliable tests will surely result.

Young children usually have to be tested individually, rather than in groups. Teachers may have to request assistance during any testing period, in order to permit completion of the planned testing program. Young children respond better to adults they know well and trust, and therefore they are best tested by their own classroom teacher or by some well-known and well-liked school official or by someone who is professionally competent and is willing to spend the time needed to establish trust and rapport.

It is important to avoid subjecting children to long or too-frequent tests. This means careful selection of concepts to test and a test structure which can yield profitable data, within a minimum period of time. Teachers who know young children are aware of their semantic difficulties and realize that test questions must be clearly and simply worded, that instructions must be concise and as fool-proof as possible, and that, wherever possible, children should be required to respond in nonverbal or performance ways.

Some examples of the test items used in the two studies described in this book will be found in the Appendices. These were not paper-and-pencil tests, which most teachers think of when tests are mentioned. Neither did all of the test items require verbal responses from the child. It can be seen that young children's intellectual learnings can be tested in innumerable ways, providing the teacher is willing to acquire the needed background in evaluation techniques.

Interpreting Test Results

When tests have been scored, they can be listed on paper in descending or ascending order of total score, followed by or parallel with subscores on various items of the test. It can be seen immediately who the high scorers and low scorers are and who constitute the middle range. Much can be learned about the test results simply by scanning them, noting high and low scores, medians, and items which fared particularly well or poorly in the test results. Thus it can be seen which test items appeared most troublesome to the class and which received the best responses.

When teachers have any correlative or comparative data about children's achievements, or when they have studied all or most of the children to the point where they have formed some judgments about abilities and skills, they can immediately make comparisons between test results and such other information. Sometimes the test results offer surprises, indicating more ability and understanding, or less, than the teacher had supposed. However, it is often necessary to discount test results if they are in contradiction to other reliable sources of information. In the economics study, one of the lowest scorers on the test was a child who had been tested by a reputable psychologist and found to have an IQ above 170. However, attendance records showed that this child had been absent on an extended visit to a relative, with an absence rate of 80 per cent during the period of the study. In this case, it was not necessary to discount the results, since it was obvious that this very able child had missed the opportunity to learn the concepts which had been studied. This case also constituted further evidence of the substantial learning which other children had realized during the study, since the results could not have come from simple maturation or everyday experience.

It has been noted above that without using any quantitative methods at all, it is possible to learn a great deal about test results simply by studying them. However, teachers who are willing to learn more about statistical techniques, either in a college course or through other sources, will be able to use other fruitful analyses and will find it possible to construct indices which can be used for various types of comparisons and measurements. Perhaps one of the most important products of further study in evaluation is the understanding of the limitations of all methods of evaluation and of the relative tentativeness of all results.

INTRODUCING
NEW PROGRAMS

School systems and teachers eager to plan for an immediate introduction of the approach to conceptual learning proposed in this book may have to be quite experimental and adventurous in initiating changes and making their needs known. Considerable initiative may have to be exercised before scholars in some of the disciplines are able to help in this direction.

In some disciplines, a national task force composed of scholars alone or of academic scholars and educators, has formulated and issued a statement of key concepts. While such a product is authoritative and reliable, it constitutes a single one-way transmission to teachers with no facility or apparatus for evaluating the product in its practical application or for making any indicated changes or improvements. By contrast, there have been several instances in which scholars and educators have collaborated with teachers in developing experimental programs by means of a process which permits evaluation and adaptation and change. This productive approach to local experimentation with university collaboration seems destined to offer fruitful guides for all school systems and to lead to a carefully refined and well-tested product.

If changes in knowledge are to be reflected in the kindergarten, programs will have to be formulated which advance conceptual development for five-year-olds. Such programs must be designed to furnish experiences needed for initial concepts, with the understanding that many different types of experiences may lead to the attainment of the same concept. Concepts are not aggregations of facts, although facts contribute to the understanding and development of these abstractions and generalizations. Children can be guided to grapple with significant ideas in familiar and well-known settings but they need not be limited exclusively to what they can touch and see. In all cases, the teacher's guidance must be directed toward the ideas to be grasped and upon children's satisfactions in achieving knowledge. Developing a curriculum from this point of view challenges teachers to develop the considerable potential of the school in making knowledge available to children.

The authors of this book, having explored some of the possibilities of such a curriculum in separate, independent studies, are impressed with the rich potential of this approach to kindergarten content. Their own studies reflected the following findings and insights about children's intellectual learnings:

The studies demonstrated that teaching for intellectual competence is possible in a kindergarten. The children related some vital experiences to some important ideas in the social sciences. They had taken an initial, basic step in a process which would continue for many more years. Concept formation does not occur in a single learning experience but is a process that continues with each new bit of information and insight. Observational recordings and test data indicated substantial learning had occurred.

It was found that children could maintain interest in ideas over long periods of time and that children could recall experiences that occurred many weeks before. Both studies continued over a period of several months. During this time the children frequently returned to deal with the same concepts. In the literature of early childhood education teachers are generally warned that it is necessary to limit any organized sequence of learnings to a few days or a few weeks at most. Yet it was found that the extended duration of these studies was advantageous. There was no need to hurry through experiences and it was possible to return to activities and programs for reinforcement of learnings and for clarification of meanings. The same concepts could be explored in different contexts. Planning around big ideas instead of small facts freed the teacher of the need to "cover" specific details at any one time. In-depth study of ideas, rather than a "once-over-lightly," superficial approach, proved a satisfying, productive experience for five-year-olds.

The program centering on key concepts offered children opportunities to develop skills in formulating and testing hypotheses. As they observed new phenomena children used the information they had gathered from previous experiences to explain unfamiliar elements. Often the hypotheses seemed unreasonable from an adult point of view, but, as the children acquired new information and understandings, they were able to modify their hypotheses and to begin to reject inappropriate ones.

There was much evidence of conceptual learning. Data gathered during both studies and from before-and-after tests indicated that the children had accomplished more than mere factual learning. There were many examples of children's categorization, definition, and generalization. Sometimes these were erroneous due to misconceptions. Many, however, were adequate and reasonable and indicated the real meaning children had acquired.

There were many examples of children's attempt to transfer their learnings in encountering new situations. This was further evidence that the children had gone beyond collection of facts in their study of these social science areas. There was increased understanding of some of the tools of social scientists, including such symbolic representations as graphs and maps. The children's growing reservoir of facts and details, under teacher guidance and assistance, contributed to this progress.

Variety in resources was in itself a necessity for rich conceptual learning. It appeared that there was no one method or one way of studying concepts that guaranteed the success of the program. Since children varied so widely in prior experiences, understandings, and interests, variety in resources for learning furnished the novelty and stimulation needed by different children.

The concepts which the children learned best were those which were most directly focused upon in the program. Such economic concepts as the family, producers, and consumers, which were studied in a variety of ways with well-defined language experiences, were more successfully learned than other concepts which were studied indirectly or through few experiences. This finding underlines the teacher's need to plan very specifically for desired learnings.

Through discussions and other interactions with children, it was possible for the teacher to offer necessary language experiences. Words and their definitions and usage which children needed in their thinking were circulated and interchanged. It was obvious that unless children's language ability is developed along with their experiences, they are limited in their ability to use, develop and communicate ideas.

Play was an integral part of each of the programs and an essential ingredient of young children's concept development. While most of the initial learnings in both studies came from direct experiences, manipulative and dramatic play opportunities made it possible for children to explore these ideas further, to stabilize them and to make them their own. Although play did not constitute the total learning experience, it constituted an essential and indispensable part of the kindergarten program for fostering intellectual development.

The studies emphasized the important role in children's concept development of knowledgeable teachers who teach more actively and directedly than has been customary in the past. The need for skilled teacher guidance of children through play toward definition, categorization, and differentiation was clearly demonstrated in both studies. It was indicated that the path from concrete to abstract ideas may be shortened by teachers who plan for desired outcomes in ways that are meaningful for children. While the need for concrete experiences remains basic for young children's learning, more suitable manipulative materials and other types of learning tools can become worthwhile supplements.

CONCLUSIONS

The program proposed in this book for developing intellectual content in the kindergarten can only contribute to significant curriculum change as it undergoes and withstands the test of classroom use. Modifications in educational programs do not occur automatically. They are the product of extensive collaboration by many people at different levels of the educational enterprise. It is unlikely that kindergarten teachers can take the full responsibility or initiative for substantial curriculum change all by themselves. Yet there are important contributions which must come primarily from the classroom teacher if major changes in program are to be attained. Some of the ways in which teachers can encourage and contribute to such change follow:

The classroom teacher needs to evaluate her program from the point of view of the intellectual challenges available to children in her class.

A detailed appraisal by the teacher of the opportunities in her own classroom for concept development could be a very practical beginning to planning for needed changes. Are the children working toward the understanding of significant ideas? Are the children being told about ideas or are they exploring or experiencing them in some challenging forms?

There is a need to develop a greater variety of materials and equipment to enable kindergarten children to attain significant concepts before they learn to read.

Because the young child's mode of learning is mainly kinesthetic, motoric, and perceptual, materials and equipment are his tools for learning. New materials need to be developed to support and stimulate learning in the kinds of programs proposed here. Materials for measurement, for discovery, for symbolizing ideas, and for practicing the use of new concepts are necessary. Teachers will have to make known their needs for additional materials so that equipment manufacturers can develop appropriate types of instructional materials. Variety itself was shown to be productive in stimulating different children and in providing opportunities for perceptual learning, as well as in helping the teacher to expand children's horizons, interests, and understandings, in the two studies cited in this book.

Teachers can begin to test young children's ability to spend long blocks of time in learning pursuits in which they become involved.

It is time to explode the myths of the short attention span of five-year-olds and of their inability to pursue an idea or a learning situation over varying periods of time. Teachers who observe children in significant and appropriate learning situations are soon convinced that it is the program which determines the children's attention span far more often than the other way around.

The productive results of episodic learning[4] can be tested in kindergarten programs.

An episode is a learning situation. Unlike a unit, an episode is one of a series of learning situations, none of which are complete in themselves, none of which pretend to offer desired learnings to a group of children within a few days or even a few weeks, but all of which offer recurring learning situations over long periods of time. Episodic learning assumes children develop concepts gradually over substantial periods of time and that their understandings change and grow. If teachers can select some of the more significant and basic learnings goals upon which to focus, they can schedule many learning episodes during the school year, instead of trying to "cover" complex ideas in short periods of time, neatly wrapped up into "units."

Teachers need to make appraisals of the resources available to children for intellectual inquiry.

An inventory of the various facilities and materials available to the teacher for offering challenging intellectual content to her class may be helpful in making better use of what is accessible and obtainable. The teacher needs precise information on places to go on trips, sources of free and inexpensive materials, resource people in the school and in the community, as well as among the parents of the children. Teachers should also know about the kinds of materials and equipment that are available through the school system that may be ordered or borrowed, to enrich the experiences of children. Some teachers may find it useful to keep an index file of such resources according to their potential for different kinds of learning, to explore new ways of using equipment.

Teachers need to develop clear plans for children's learning which include intellectual goals.

Without specific goals, modification of elements in the learning situation would have minimal effect. Objectives and plans are needed to give direction to proposed changes and to allow for

---

[4] The authors of this book are indebted to the Series Editor, Professor Kenneth D. Wann, for the descriptive term, "episodic learning."

evaluation. Only when teachers make plans to modify purposes can they make intelligent plans to modify programs.

Teachers need to experiment with different ways of organizing for instruction.

There are many more ways of grouping children for instruction than most teachers use. Individual approaches, small group and total class divisions may have merit for various purposes and for different activities. Teachers need to explore classroom arrangements, modifying the placement of furniture and the use of space, as well as developing different time schedules for specific purposes.

Teachers need to be aware of the developing knowledge about what children can learn and how they learn.

Recently psychologists have turned their attention to the cognitive aspects of development. New research promises significant insights and contributions to the content and methodology of early childhood education. Teachers need to seek more information and practical guides from psychologists in the area of learning in young children.

Teachers need to involve other people in curriculum change.

Isolated innovation is difficult and unnecessary. Teachers interested in change need to muster support and interest among their colleagues, supervisors, and administrators. A well-reasoned statement of the need for change is likely to receive sympathetic treatment in any school. Teachers also need to invite academic scholars to work jointly on committees or to act as resource persons in the development of new educational programs. Scholars can contribute to the continuous process of clarifying and updating the content of young children's school experiences.

Teachers need to communicate what takes place in the classroom.

In the past many misconceptions developed around the kindergarten because of lack of information. Teachers need to explore more effective means of communication than they have had. It is important for teachers to share ideas and to test each other's ideas in varying situations, and therefore kindergarten teachers need better communication with other kindergarten teachers. Primary teachers must be aware of the kindergarten program, to develop realistic expectations for children, and to effectuate better articulation than in the past. Supervisors and administrators, often uninformed about the kindergarten and early childhood education generally, need to become informed of needs and changes in prospect. Parent groups and the general public must also be better informed, so that understanding and support may begin to replace some of the current criticism and lack of information. Significant kindergarten programs can only grow out of positive teacher response to proposals for change, supported and facilitated by the school and the community.

BIBLIOGRAPHY

Almy, Millie, *Ways of Studying Children*, New York: Teachers College Press, Teachers College, Columbia University, 1959.

Anastasi, Anne, *Psychological Testing*, New York: Macmillan, 1961.

Bloom, Benjamin S. (Ed.), *Taxonomy of Educational Objectives: The Classification of Educational Goals,* Handbook I: Cognitive Domain, New York: David McKay, 1956.

Buros, Oscar K. (Ed.), *The Fifth Mental Measurements Yearbook*, Highland Park, N.J.: Gryphon Press, 1959.

Cohen, Dorothy H., and Virginia Stern, *Observing and Recording the Behavior of Young Children*, New York: Teachers College Press, Teachers College, Columbia University, 1958.

Gerberich, J. Raymond, Harry A. Greene, and Albert N. Jorgensen, *Measurement and Evaluation in the Modern School*, New York: David McKay, 1962.

Green, John A., *Teacher-Made Tests*, New York: Harper and Row, 1963.

Jersild, Arthur T., *Child Psychology* (5th ed.), Englewood Cliffs, N.J.: Prentice-Hall, 1960.

Lindvall, C. M., *Testing and Evaluation: An Introduction*, New York: Harcourt, Brace and World, 1961.

Noll, Victor H., *Introduction to Educational Measurement*, Boston: Houghton Mifflin, 1957.

Thomas, R. Murray, *Judging Student Progress*, New York: Longmans, Green, 1960.

Thorndike, Robert L., and Elizabeth Hagen, *Measurement and Evaluation in Psychology and Education* (2nd ed.), New York: John Wiley and Sons, 1961.

Townsend, Edward Arthur, and Paul J. Burke, *Statistics for the Classroom Teacher*, New York: Macmillan, 1963.

Wrightstone, J. Wayne, Joseph Justman, and Irving Robbins, *Evaluation in Modern Education*, New York: American Book, 1956.

APPENDICES

A. EXAMPLES OF TEST ITEMS USED IN THE ECONOMIC STUDY

1. *Concept of "producer,"* in the sense in which economists use the term, that is, someone who works and who produces either goods or services.

Each child was shown three pictures which he was told were producers and three which he was told were not. The details of the pictures were discussed. The child was told each group of these pictures "went together," that one group was called producers, while the other was not. The child was asked to define "producer" and to name another producer, and these were, of course, verbal responses. Then the child was given a stack of ten pictures and he was asked to sort them into two piles, with either of the two groups previously shown. After the child sorted the pictures, he was asked in each case for the same three pictures, why the picture belonged to the pile to which it had been assigned.

These test items explored the child's ability to differentiate producers from nonproducers without offering any verbal response, to formulate a definition or generalization in words and finally to indicate his ability to think logically in explaining why several pictures belonged to the category he had chosen. A good test should be constructed so that more than one level of conceptual learning can be simultaneously ascertained, so that the child who finds difficulty in verbal expression can use some form of nonverbal or manipulative reaction and, in addition, so that developing language ability can also be sampled.

2. *Concept of money.* The child's understanding of, and ability to

identify, money was tested by giving him a small purse containing a check, a dollar bill, a quarter, a dime, a nickel, and a penny. The child was asked to state what this was, what it was used for, and how people got it. He was also asked to identify each piece of money.

This question tested the child's ability to state his conception of the uses of money and how money is obtained, as well as the simpler matter of identifying and naming money. Again, there were two levels tested: one factual and enumerative, the other requiring definition and generalization.

3. *Concepts about families, family income, and jobs.* The child was given a box containing a family of dolls to play with and manipulate, to tell stories about, and to answer questions about. The questions related to his understandings about variation in family size and composition, about which members of families work and what kinds of jobs they do and about limitations of family income.

B. EXAMPLES OF TEST ITEMS USED IN THE GEOGRAPHY–HISTORY STUDY

1. *Definitions.* (a) The child was asked to define various terms introduced into the vocabulary in the course of studying New York Harbor. Word definitions were asked for such terms as harbor, dock, channel, freighter and cargo. (b) Vocabulary and definitions were also elicited from children by showing them objects, such as a small model of a harbor or of an ocean liner, or pictures, and asking them, for example, to name the object and to explain its use.

2. *Map concepts.* The child was shown a New York City map and was asked various questions designed to test his understanding of map concepts, such as the use of blue coloring to designate water areas, and the use of lines to denote roads and streets.

3. *Historical change.* The child's understandings of changes in time were tested by asking him to differentiate between models of modern and older or ancient objects, such as boats, and to indicate which were still in use.